# SINGING
## AT THE GATES

# SINGING
# AT THE GATES
## Selected Poems

### JIMMY SANTIAGO BACA

Grove Press
*New York*

*Printed in the United States of America*
*Published simultaneously in Canada*

ISBN: 978-0-8021-2210-0
eBook ISBN: 978-0-8021-9290-5

Grove Press
an imprint of Grove/Atlantic, Inc.
154 West 14th Street
New York, NY 10011

Distributed by Publishers Group West

www.groveatlantic.com

14 15 16 17   10 9 8 7 6 5 4 3 2 1

*for Stacy*

# CONTENTS

# Author's Note

Early through my prison sentence for drug possession I began writing Mariposa. She too was a poet, with three books to her credit, but that wasn't the kernel of my inspiration. No indeed, she had agreed to let me write her with all my questions on what a woman needed, dreamed of, felt, probing the very vaults of woman's sexual secrets. And, of course, in blind heat I flung myself into this joyous undertaking and soon my letters were fat volumes of contrition and vows to love her forever. O, that every young poet should have someone like her on the receiving end of their poems, someone who levies no judgments, no academic critiques. She responded with passionate encouragement to just write, write, and write. And I did and in such manner was I able to explore my deepest fears and most naive assumptions and improve not only my mind and my imagination but also my writing. I let go as avidly as the gullet crowing of a rooster at dawn.

And thus this collection begins by reaching back to those early days when I was learning how to write and read and continues on to spread its

literary wings over the past four decades, and fi-
nally perches on a branch of the present day.

It covers a lot of distance, whirling in a spec-
trum of varied themes from prison reform, love,
education, barrio life, environmental issues, and
the joys of family. Ranging from short to long lines,
logic grounded in the hearty senses to surreal land-
scapes of the imagination, terse metaphors to un-
folding multilayered verse, outraged to serene,
playful, compassionate, and exploratory.

I love the growl of poetry, the staggering crash
of idols and the burning of literary pacifiers. I love
the breakthrough to spiritual development of self
that rattles the cage of fear and frees you to become
more of yourself through embracing life, its sorrows
and enchantments. And that's what these poems call
for, incinerating our convenient complacency that
has allowed our environment to become so toxic
we can't breathe the air, drink the water, or eat the
food. This collection is by no means timid. These
poems are about risk taking and losing all you have,
stripping yourself of the unessential detritus that
accumulates through artificial culture and going
lightly into the adventure of life—bare ass naked
as the day you were born.

I look back at those initiate days, between
1973 and 1979, when I was a young man in Ari-
zona in a maximum-security prison, and I sing
joyous praise for the cage and the guards and the
warden. Thank you for condemning me to a 5x8
cell for over six years; had I not been imprisoned
at a time when my youthful fervor was to slake

my thirst at the elicit nectar of the criminal tit, I would have been killed or murdered by the cops or DEA. But instead I live, and I live to write these poems another day.

Interspersed through the collection are poems originally published in various magazines and journals, poems that represent my first jaunt into the public eye. And, I might add, my first payment—for some of the poems I received a mere ten dollars, which to me at the time seemed like a million because the lift in confidence that gave me was immeasurable.

I chose the epistolary format to start communicating with the world and friends, and writing letters for me became the outlet I was most comfortable with in laying out my emotions and thoughts. I mixed poetry and prose not from choice but necessity. I needed a wide-open field page, something broad, an expanse in which to seed my words, to be allowed to expand my train of thought, to track my doubts and acclaim my certainties.

To be sure, my teachers were as strange as footprints on the ceiling. These early love letters to Mariposa got my body purring and my heart rumbling. I was also writing letters for the convicts, killers, and gangsters—they often asked me to write their wives, girlfriends, kids, etc. Then Will Inman, an old gay white man living in Tucson, good souled, heart brimming with justice for all, launched me on a poetic-activism adventure that had me reading Ernesto Cardenal

(Nicaragua) and Miguel Hernández (Spain), to name a couple, and writing reams of letters. Beginning in 1977, Will and I exchanged over a hundred letters within a period of six months—some of my letters were published in *Illuminations*, his bilingual magazine established along the Arizona/Mexico border.

Assailing the days with such enthusiasm and adrenaline as I had never done, driven by the stimulus of a linguistic universe hitherto unimagined, I blew away the margins and perimeters of all that I had known or assumed in my pre-poetry days. When you get arrested and convicted of selling drugs and they accuse you of attempted murder on a DEA agent and take you out on the West Side prairie at four a.m. and try to push you out of a car going 60 mph and, failing this, break your jaw with a gun butt and cheekbones with a fist, and your front teeth are gone and you come to in the hospital—it's a wake-up call for most but a special one if you're a poet.

Imagine you're sitting at home in a house you built that contains all you have in life. Suddenly, a sheriff breaks through the door and hollers, *You got one minute to get out.* And a minute later you're standing outside on the road watching your house and everything in it consumed by fire. You have sixty seconds to grab everything that means something to you. Most people snatch up family photos and rush out.

That's what writing was for me, every day—snatching memories and writing them down before the fire of forgetfulness and trauma relegated them to the dark chambers of amnesia. When I got put in prison, everything burned before me and I stood and watched it burn down. No vestiges or tangible links to my past, lean from loss, I went through my memories and started scaling and trimming and editing to revive them from the ashes. In a manner of speaking, that's what this collection is about—the salvaged remains of my life, always one step ahead of the fire that blows through my imagination. I write from this place of immediate evacuation, from a place where I must leave everything behind and take only what I can carry and what is most meaningful to me—and that is the narrative, the story, the poem.

Timing is everything.

My very first chapbook, *Rockbook 3*, was part of the publisher's series called the *Rock Bottom Books*. Having my first chapbook published was like stumbling onto a freshwater spring in the mountains and finding intact Anasazi pottery bowls to drink from. I went there for water, came back with priceless discoveries of cultural significance. In a violent setting like prison, any artifact that affirms your humanity is invaluable and that's what the chapbook did. Even though it was humble in design and origin, it affirmed my worth and purpose as a human being and not just a prisoner with a number. Hell, for the first few days I thought I was Norman Mailer or Grace Paley.

It was the greatest beginning a poet could have. I mean, imagine, living in a place where men were stripped down to their essential cores, screams of torturous madness crackling the midnight air, human beings split in two by rapists, killers beheading other criminals, everyone on guard, everyone operating and existing on hope, deteriorating into despair, the strong broken, every bond that kept these men intact rendered insufficient in holding the opposing forces of life and death in balance, everyone swept over the ravaging waterfalls of sheer survival and in the process becoming the person they most feared they might become. What a magnificent place to set a poet to record the human soul! And there I was, witness to the human landscape under epic conflict. Instead of sitting in the day-care nurseries of dreary university classrooms, I was gifted to be an eyewitness to life on the edge.

And around the time of 1975, an amazing stranger in Santa Barbara, California, solicited my poems and later published a small chapbook, entitled *Swords of Darkness*. I was beside myself, enthralled, drunk on the elixir of becoming a *known* poet. (Where are you, my friend? Thank you for this gift in my development as a poet that has meant so much to me.)

My work with words, like a blacksmith on his anvil, was slowly breaking the tangible attachments to my criminal and illiterate past and creating—through writing and language and reading books—a paradigm shift. No longer bound in the mummy wrappings of illiteracy, in *Rockbook 3* and *Swords of Darkness* and in the dozens of magazine poems and in Will Inman's anthology *Illuminations,* I began to lock on to what the potential of my life might become by using language the way a person lost in the wilderness takes his compass to steer him in a direction he senses will guide him to fulfill his destiny. You can understand how I so appreciated the altruism of strangers who published my poems and the little endearing chapbooks—a backbreaking undertaking—printed on an old mimeograph machine, sheets of paper folded in half and stapled.

Then in 1982—now in freedom—*What's Happening* was published by Curbstone Press, my first commercial poetry book, a turning-point book that crystallized my fate as a poet in the world. Just as many remember where they were during horrible catastrophes: bombed skyscrapers, hurricanes, assassinations, in my case, as with many poets, I remember the place and time I wrote the poems for my first "real" book from an independent press. I was in Blacksburg, Virginia, staying in an upstairs room in an old Victorian mansion long past its prime, next to a Civil War cemetery, so cold I burned the furniture to keep from freezing since I didn't have money for fuel. And yet despite my poverty, shivering bones, and lack of food and basic essentials for living, I was happier than I had ever been. I was careful to steer clear of the assembly-line formulaic poem, whose verse is groomed and combed out line after line, cozied in stanzas like the twine on a hangman's rope, slowly choking life and breath out of language. Through this book a light had suddenly appeared, illuminating my life—a certain radiance umbrella'd the days ahead when I thought about my future. I wasn't making any money at all but I was happy, the kind of quiet peace one feels when finally moving into a home with a roommate you love: poetry was my roommate for life.

After over a decade of writing and publishing poetry books, I returned to my roots and wrote a collection to support Cedar Hill Publishers in San Diego, a small nonprofit, run by the indomitable Maggie Jasper and edited by CP, a prisoner at the Corcoran correctional facility in California. You might say I partnered with a criminal. Maggie had written me asking if I would give her a chapbook to help the press get on its feet financially. It was a young independent press struggling to make it, and because small presses played a large roll in my poetic development I readily agreed.

*Set This Book on Fire!* was published in 1999 and edited by a man doing time in prison—an applicable irony aimed at those who use humor to demean hardship and suffering. To the privileged, any writing about suffering should be kept under lock and key in a steel box in the basement. Of course, *Set This Book on Fire!* disentitled them and made them mad, ill at ease. These poems flatten the tires of the status quo's funeral hearse with its cadavers muttering the same old, same old scapegoat complaints against the criminal class.

Soon my humble fame brought new requests from painters, photographers, and filmmakers working on projects that rallied against that same status quo. James Drake asked me to write poems for his transvestite photographs from his La Brisa collection. Norman Mauskopf, the famed photographer from Santa Fe, asked me to write a long poem to accompany his photographs of northern New Mexico Chicano culture, and Kathryn Ferguson offered me the opportunity of writing a long narrative poem for her documentary *Rita of the Sky.*

It was a wonderful way for me to dive into the long narrative and these were themes I appreciated —bicultural for Drake, Chicano life for Mauskopf, and judicial issues for Ferguson. At the time I was living in an apartment by the Rio Grande. It was a time of reckoning and regeneration—to change, live by kinder and healthier choices, connect with Mother Earth in a deeper spiritual way—and in doing so become a better person, more substantial and purposeful, ridding myself of detrimental habits and morphing into a higher being.

Every morning, whether it was freezing or raining or windy, in the most inclement weather, reluctant or otherwise, I rose with the sun and went jogging along the river. And with every week that passed into months, I resensitized my heart and soul to the environment's lovely kernels of wisdom; I aligned my feelings to appreciate the birds, water, air, noting the subtle significance of colors and textures around me from the tiniest grass tendrils and buds to the birth of mallard ducklings wiggling behind their waddling mother in *la acequia.*

I would stand for minutes mesmerized by the sun on my brow and cheeks, a plumage of soft heat feathering my flesh, watching the combat between sun sparks glimmering off ditch water. I was even lucky enough one time to catch sight of two blue heron feathers floating in a nest of twigs drifting in the center of the water. I waded out, thighs carving through the current, and I carefully cradled them in my palms and wrapped them in my T-shirt and carried them home.

Acutely aware of my surroundings, I birthed a consciousness in me that brought about an abundance of detail heretofore unnoticed; new life now teemed and abounded in my ears, eyes, and nose.

I kept thinking of that woman named Rita, a Rarámuri Indian, charged with killing her husband in Chihuahua, Mexico. She fled and crossed the desert and was found years later in an alley in Kansas City rummaging in a dumpster for food. I carried her with me on every run. Her intelligence imbued me, shaped my hours, my mind filled with her figure walking in the desert, under the hot Sonoran sun. I tried to feel and sense what she might have felt and sensed as she trekked across the burning sands.

Once found, she was kept in an asylum for the mentally ill for years until one day a nurse, escorting a new doctor down the hallway, pointed to Rita in a cell and said the woman was insane, babbling in strange tongues, and no one knew who she was or where she came from. And because there was so little known about her, the hospital staff and authorities referred to her as Rita of the Sky. The visiting doctor touring the facility, however, hailed from the same region in Chihuahua, Mexico, and he cried out that it was no nonsensical babble but a language he was fluent in. Through this doctor's efforts, it was discovered that Rita was not crazy and never had been.

After legal hearings with court-appointed lawyers petitioning in her behalf Rita was discharged. She was awarded a million dollars in damages but the lawyers kept most of it, giving Rita a paltry sum of one thousand dollars. After her release, old and decrepit, she returned to her village where she spent the rest of her days. In my poem, "Rita Falling from the Sky," I try to conjure those interminable miles she roamed, over hostile terrain and forbidding landscape, to arrive in Kansas.

I was hardly able to catch my breath after my expedition into the desert with Rita when Drake reached out to me to write something to accompany a photography exhibit at the Whitney Museum in New York. I dropped everything and said *Yes*. Simplified, the photos were of transvestite prostitutes working in a border cantina. I knew La Frontera well enough, the Ciudad Juárez and Las Cruces border, as I had been going down there since I was a kid, smuggling a load or two of marijuana across that very border.

The photographs touched a nerve. Chicanos are a hybrid culture, Indio-euro, born when the first Native American woman was raped or loved by the invading marauders from Europe. Thus, the Mestizo was born. I am Indio-euro or, in my own Chicano assignation, Mestizo-Genazaro, and that ethnic split in my heritage and genetic makeup gives me a certain insight into the gender split of these men. Because I am bicultural, the project piqued my intrigue as transvestites also are composed of two opposing parts—female personalities trapped in male bodies. And while Indio-euro is my bloodline, Chicanismo is my soul and culture. This identity is informed by an American life in general but also by one who has done prison time. And a day after I talked to Drake on the phone, FedEx dropped off a packet stuffed with photographs. They were magnificent.

This psychic split was a theme I wanted to explore and without wasting a second I spread the photos across the floor and studied them one by one and tried to respond to them. I followed the contours of each erotic body, trying to read their suppressed pain through their attitude, decipher their sexualized eyes and painted faces, and interpret my own feelings about my own mixed ethnic makeup. It went quickly. The lurid and vulgar portraits suggested secrets to reveal. My job was to fling open the portals of their strange and eerie world. Their images—at once vulnerable and defiant as corner prostitutes, the flammable poses and dark features and spiked high heels and sparkle of their cheap lipstick, nail polish, and black fishnet nylons—doused my interest with combustible fuel that exploded in me. They stared at me from the photos as if I was their hostage, gripped by their sorrowful hands and legs. I wrote through the night into the next afternoon, lifting the veil of each male victim dressed as a woman, who would all eventually be murdered or die from drug overdoses. By the end of the following day I was stuffing first-draft poems into a FedEx pack to be overnighted to Drake.

My piece was titled "Smoking Mirrors," and the exhibit was popular enough that the University of Washington published my poem and Drake's photographs into a book to commemorate our collaboration. The book is entitled *Que Linda La Brisa* (La Brisa being the name of a transvestite cantina in La Zona, the red-light district in Ciudad Juárez, Mexico).

After that, and still feeling the injustice done to these people, I was more than willing to lose myself in another project that might absorb me to such an extent that I could separate myself from that bitter reality on the border. I had been depressed for weeks when my friend the photographer Norman Mauskopf walked into my house. This man's got more balls than a herd of bulls and an eye to capture the essence of his subjects that rides the highest rails of creativity. He asked me to compose a long poem to accompany his photographic history of northern New Mexico Chicano culture.

The result is "Singing at the Gates." Whimsical in style, nostalgic, and contemporary in tone, it is a simple celebration of Chicano culture, a sort of pencil drawing of myself in myriad forms, sketched in metaphors and images and lyrical language. More symbolic than practical, here is a personal myth that blows my heart-seed hopes and dreams over the land where I grew up and still inhabit, in freedom and in the ideal faith that I will have a life free from the yoke of oppression and imprisonment I experienced for twenty-five years.

This poem carries a lot of primal significance for me, a pivotal memorial to my liberation from the shackles of illiteracy by teaching myself to read and write in prison. It is sometimes fierce and compassionate in its commitment to overcome day-to-day adversity, an outraged dystopian cry for La Plebe to rise and demand their rights be respected, merging genres to achieve something larger than me.

To conclude this collection, I include recent poems that connect to the plight of people struggling against the oppression of class, of poverty, of apathy, and the struggles of war. In a way these poems bring us around to the beginning of the collection—where the fight for self, dignity, and meaning rages against man-made boundaries and larger-than-life obstacles.

The poems collected here express not only the four decades of my journey, but also the journeys of other lives that parallel my own battles, hopes, aspirations, and dreams. From inside the walls that hold us and divide us, language has the means of breaking through into light, love, freedom, and celebration of life. All of us experience conflict with joy and pain. All of us with genuine voices— not scarecrow mimicry that borrows and copies— create a sublime journey to find beauty in what is considered the mundane.

# SINGING
## AT THE GATES

## Excerpts from the Mariposa Letters

22
I am like the colorful Quetzal Bird
glowing rich and heavy
flung wings splattering against early skies
my cries dripping like red paint on the white
   horizons

23
I handle the glittering diamond-hilt of hate daily
and decide what to do

24
memories tangle up in trees like gigantic
   cobwebs

25
and the winds sputtered their jowls like horses
wrenching the wretched roots of me

26
you walk in robes of the world's moonlight
around you like a ghostly nightgown
you blood-burning witch and queen cat
purring with your womb lips

27
carrying the echoes of our dreams
that grit their teeth along my bones nightly
and hammer along my heart for a secret passage

28
I realize prison is but another name for a long
    long night
in which the one you most love is absent

*

35
This morning
still half asleep beneath my blankets
I'd brush your hair with my fingers
rub your flanks down
following over your hips
down sleek firm lengths of your thigh,

                    more than this:
the warmth I'd feel in my heart
the many things I have done in this life

all settled now like residue
asleep in the honey feeling of morning
as I touched you.

36
When leaves spin through the air
like green diamonds, I have always felt
the need to put my pants on,
tie my boots on, don a loose cotton shirt
and go walking, breathing in and out
tramping great distances
on the side of the road
as cars passed to and from.

37
I have begun to speak a new language.
With you, I touch on words I never knew existed.
I can't vocalize them, but within me
a whole land of people have finally found
their mother tongue
and now I feel I belong, finally with meaning
at the root of each word
that little red dictionary
I leaf through hour by hour now
amazed at the wealth of language

38
I feel like a child with you, woman
learning love, slowly writing out my feelings
in big letters across the sky
and able to touch your heart like a leaf

39
We are children. And you and I
always amazed
by the immeasurable found in flowers
or the gold in sunny days
or the kingdoms we see in the moon.
They say our dreams are not real. They say
there the real world.
We look at each other and smile.
I hug you because your slippers are made
of mooncloth when you step to kiss me.

40
We are like the butterfly and hummingbird;
we have felt hurt a million times like buckshot in
   our wings

41
My thoughts surface for air
almost frightened and angry
then the thoughts return
swimming upstream to breeding grounds
to the clear pebbly-blue shallows of my heart.

42
I somehow find someone sitting on porch stoops
   with the same mind
as mine, and we find laughter, tears, stories
we each dream a woman, and if that dream is
   broken,
each man breaks inside himself, his life becomes
   a long

feverish tribal dance, his days haze
in the flurry of bongo hands
while his neck and head shake and fling
to sweet sad music, no longer slow,
his pulses like piano keys plink and tum
squeak and ring
the dream between his jaws
chewed like cocaine on his long swirling inward
  journey,
veins twisting up tight and knotted
the wrist dangling and wrenched and snapped
  into clapping
as the song goes on, of man without woman

*


51
Woman, speaking about when my cock
enters, plunges the far wells of your womb,
I will tell what I want,
what secrets I wish to come forth
from my questioning cock, nosing deep
into your still water, rippling the silent blue
silver, the water surface
in the jungly jeweled depths of your womb
struck with my sunlight, quivering with my
drumming balls

I want your hips to shake
like a fish flapping out of water
your hips slapping and whipping
from side to side

as if your womb lips were gills
sucking feverishly at my oxen-thick cock
prodding you, your womb unfolding
like a butterfly from the golden petal of the
   afternoon,
to flick wings quickly
as if dancing on air your buttocks swishing
grinding trance-like
not a second still, jiggling the soft loins
of your legs, lathering love honey between
our legs, under and down our legs dripping

explode for me woman in furious waves and
   lashes
a thousand times a minute sweep and rip
your hips, your ass, your pelvis into me
like a wild mare in a stall of fire
unleashing your groans and snarls
your cunt clawing and grabbing
for more male cock, King Lord of woman's flesh,
woman devour and plunder me

52
I take your flesh in my hands
each caress a small delicate string
I pluck slowly then speed my fingers through
your legs meander along the bed sheets
my fingers play expresses to your body
plucking fast and

running my fingers across
your breasts as if they were nights
your nipples moons and my hands huge wings

plucking our song
your whimperings
my sweet elongated mumbles

*

56
Dressed in peasant skirt, Spanish dancer dress
Mexican blouse, garters, black panties and
    stockings,
perfumes, diamonds, shoes with slender straps,
    woman!
you rise for all my needs,
all I ever wanted in a woman with feathers and
    beads and paint
my fingers smoldering embers
from our night's fire
all your coves and caves, all my mountains and
    plains,
your coves filled with my flooding waters,
your caves with my bones and meat, my plains
with your ploughs and crumbled dirt clods,
mist everywhere, our bodies move slowly,
never leaving the other's touch, filling in and
    nestled
in each other's curves, licking your arms, you
    kiss and caressing
with your lips my loins, your beloved man
as it was meant to be dear woman, woman,
    woman, woman . . .

*

62
I feel much like a fisherman with his plate
of hard biscuit and cold fish before him

63
How far will a man go and what is he to do
in the face of truth that doesn't even look like
    truth
but feels hidden inside somewhere
like wild animals gnawing away on prehistoric
    bones?
I've hidden deep within me that kind of truth,
the kind that snarls when you come too close to
    it.

\*

77
Though in prison, though I rage at times at the
    ignorance
and stupidity and coarseness and cruelty
behind bars, at keepers and kept,
I turn to you filling the air that I breathe
air churned darkly and heavy with steep systems
and though I say nothing,
walking early through prison mornings
my voice you hear cannot be drowned out
because by you giving me your great
spaces of love and filling them with my love,
my voice cannot be drowned out
over flooding the banks or prison
seeping into its dark dungeon hell-holes

bursting those hell-holes like dams frothing with
    light,
with my unrelenting cry of love and hope,
with my being in the very air entwining with
    yours
like stuff that falls from moon and enchants
    roots
like stuff that falls from sun soaking buds to
    bloom
that stuff is our love flowing through air
to cultivate wild the rocky regions of roses
    burgeoning
now, this very moment, as I write
this to you woman.

\*

85
Construction men finished the other side
of the dormitory, and I'm sitting here
basking in the slamming noise of gates
and I'm sitting here
thinking hopefully that the other side of the
    dormitory
will be better, it's painted pale white
and got new sinks and showers
and I'm sitting here thinking I'll get a bunk
by the window so the morning sun
will shine in on me
and maybe the guys won't blast their tv's
and stereos, maybe I won't have fools living next
    to me

at six o'clock in the morning screeching out
    their icy noise
and I'm sitting here thinking all this

when the gate at my back opens,
a few construction men walk in, hard hatted,
dusty clothed and they start hooking up this
    thing,
slip an old rubber orange hose through a
    triangle
cut into the screen that separates us from the
    guards,
and they begin to hook this hose up
ten feet away from me,

and outside I hear this rumble start up
and loud sputters pat! pat! spit! spit-pat!
and the orange hose bloats up like a python
coupled to this thing of steel
they clamp a huge chisel

one hard hatted mug grabs a shovel and stands
next to his wheelbarrow
and the other grabs this thing like a gatling gun
and hell breaks open with loud crunches and
    blasting
at the granite floor,

and beneath my feet the granite shudders,
and dry bits of cement mortar squeezed
between the granite bricks begin to crumble
    under the jackhammer

and I see our washbasins crack off the wall
and dead bugs begin falling from windowsills

clouds of dust sunset everywhere
bits of rock fly everywhere
ten feet away and they act like there ain't nobody
 here
scribbling out this poem in the dust
collecting on this page

and ten feet away they're jack blubbering granite
spitting dust in my ears and chips of rock graze
 my cheek,
and I carry on rejoicing in my humanity, singing.

*

86
my pulses like spent bullets burn in my breath
 gradually

87
so many faces in me lie dead
and so many untruths crawl without arms and
 legs

88
I sit here now
and watch the many faces of men
scuttle up from their black dark dens
I see so many come from hiding places
and now that I have finished my spiritual battle

and am strong enough, have survived my own
   weaknesses
I sit here at the portals of a destroyed being
and everything is calm, a tender lawlessness rules
and now my first step is a step of a breathing
   man
who has the grace of a wild beast
and I sit here, watching the world, the prison
and find I am richly blessed with
so many things to find out, to touch and hear
with so many men in rags and broken souls
who crawl up with dusty shoes from gutters
and carry blades in their pockets
but they are flowers that have survived their
   thorns
in dry baked ground
and I see them and I am strong enough to hear
   them
and I raise myself from contemplation and walk
toward them, to learn their language of sorrows
that hold songs like stars in their heart
songs that tell of lives and feelings that have
   been stomped on and drowned
songs are the magic that keeps men alive when
   nothing else will

I begin to sing to them
and my song is that they must sing
as I step forward, onward
through a throng of thorny men
leading them, taking them with me.

89

I carried the vulgar and wrinkled truths
I had found in the badlands of the cursed and
  exiled
and fingered them like old coins
and found they were worthless in this land
that loved money and chained children with lies

90

I have silenced my poetry and tongue to hear
  the clear
screams in the night of men slicing their throats
of victims being beaten by men I know,
of the clanging of prison gates and voices of
  tyranny
while writing my poetry I have met dark eyes.

91

someday the muscles of the universe
shall convulse into orgasm and beauty

92

And like a cat when streets become empty
in the darkness I sprang silently
through broken windows to sing what I learned

\*

107

woman, your letters are like those rocky streams
  one meets on a long journey

and I open the envelope as I might brush aside a
   bough of heavy branches
and come upon a clearing of flower and soft
   grass

108
how your voice runs clambering over the smell
   of my sweating male flesh

*

112
I will tickle you and tell you secrets of strange
   lands that shine in me
and you will caress my muscles as if they are
   wings
and I will place feathers with leather strings in
   your hair
and the lock of hair you have given me I will
   wear around my neck
my pendant made with eagle claws
and pieces of wood that click and clatter softly
   lifting against my breast as I run
and run and run
a singer with flights of birds

113
I am a little boy gone mad on the aromas of
   earth
enchanted by women whose bodies are like deep
   bass drums
that call me to sing and dance, my tongue the
   sun's spear

114
I would have known me in my disguise

115
the first green sprouts of corn jutted upward
in the dry dirt of my flesh

116
dreams flew into my fields
of my heart like great green-plumed birds
with dark eyes burning burning
as they pecked at strewn kernels of corn

and I climbed the temple steps
to the open square below where creatures
    gathered
and I reached the altar
where I lit the four torches
that threw light to the four directions
I blew away the ashes on the stone,
placed my heart there and when the sun
    touched it
it struck up, bursting in high flames exulting in
    their renewal
and with the holy fire I molded myself feathers
like the prophets made themselves scrolls and
    wrote holy words
so I made myself rich green and red and blue
    plumes
and golden light sprayed in me
and spreading my wings I flew and in my flight
were the holy words, alive and each moment was
    a holy one

like a temple with its fires
and I was the fire of sky and flaming as the earth

117
if only I could open my palm and show the
    world the diamonds of my heart

*

130
I will be leaving this place
where mad hermits laugh from yellow teeth
and crush black bugs between their fingers in
    the middle of the night
where convicts scout the silence like wicked
    pirates
their scarred faces, some have lost an eye or half
    a finger
tattoos on their arms and legs and back and
    breast—
spider webs, skulls and the Reaper, always the
    reaper
and screams of the long dead still night
still hang here like webs in the corner of the
    ceiling
and pulses crawl like black spiders with a red
    diamond on the belly
life times are spun from silk that burns easily in
    the moonlight
where so many condemn themselves for the sin
    of being born

131
I would like to rest, by a stream
take off my bandana and wet it, then dab my
  brown rough face
and place it again sopping wet around my neck
by a stream where one could hear the church
  bells beat deeply
and where one can hear birds take off through
  the branches.
For a long time I watch a line of red ants
  crawling up a tree.
I lie naked and sleep so very long
the farmland turns to city
the quiet into car horns
the stream into an asphalt road
and whoever I might have been
must know who I am, a man behind bars.


*


138
Inside the letter was a lock of your hair,
taped to the sixth page.
I caressed it
as though it were alive,
I smelled it
and ran my lips across it,
then gently
with my forefinger
caressed the hazel strands
and now I understand how
an enchanted young man is led off into the
  woods

by secret voices of tales.
I understand how he might have encountered a
    woman's hair.

\*

141
Your letters arrive, holy, bounding with claws
    into the heated earth
tearing free of the valleys, they rise into the
    mountains,
snarl from branches, sniff at the high ascents of
    rock and crawl the crevices
and scrunch through crisp leaves newly fallen,
through rivers newly gushing
then shake their fur and tramp, tongue loose, in
    long strides they push through the night and
    bound over ravines
they come here to me, the letters
they arrive and place their paws upon my chest
they curl next to me
while I listen long into the night

142
small birds whistle to me as I go hunting

143
Sunday morning.
Only one thing matters.
I wait like a small rabbit hidden in a cluster of
    bushy leaves.
I wait, there is nothing to do but wait

in the transparency of the days and sip the
   nothingness slowly
as I grow toward that day
as I'm carried toward that day.
In the blue depths of night I kick off the damp
   sweaty sheets
and lie awake, waiting
with taut readiness to spring for the day
I wait for the day when I will leave.
That day is a seed, yet to bloom.
But tell me, someone.
What is one to do waiting for a day
that is likened to God? How does one meet it?


144
I wear the moon like yanked out roots glowing
   orange
in my heart's fangs as I search for secrets in my
   life


145
By the black gates of each night
I sit, glancing at the lights of the city
listening to night talkers
and pick up the scrapings of their lives


146
the day comes
and each morning I look off
searching the ground
for its coming, checking the walls and clouds
and sense how the sun becomes hotter
how the sidewalks crack hair-thin

and grass tips forward in the breeze
everything seems to crawl out of hiding
in the death of who I was, I sing
the highest notes I reach, singing as never
  before
a bright blooded fervor
incanting in my silence
the burning wreckage as an offering of my past
in this waiting that has become a temple

\*


169
I talk with old haggard veterans of prison
and looking at their wrinkles and tired eyes
and think how much I love you
I talk with warriors here who live by the knife
and as they speak of death and danger
I think how much I love you
I pass men lying on their bunks and say
hey Reggie, hey Marvin, hey Clifford
and think how much I love you
Ole Willie sits quietly on this bunk next to mine
and makes little cards for me to send you
I share my cigarettes and coffee with him
at forty years old he is still afraid to sleep
and stays awake with me late until the night
under my night lamp I write you letters
and think of Willie and how loneliness keeps
  him up;
we say nothing all night in our little worlds
and I think how much I love you

and feel your arms around my shoulders
your hands rubbing my neck
I close my eyes and your face appears
and no matter where I walk
nothing changes
I think how much I love you.

\*

183
I pause to unbutton my shirt, looking into this
   paper
as if readying for a long walk

184
Mondays in the joint take on a different tone
   than other days.
Mondays the laundry lines seem longer
and those in line more apt to play and fuck
   around
Monday is the day when you look into your
   podner's face
eyes meeting, and for a second gazing
   searchingly those eyes
and wondering what really they are saying,
and you both seem to see a hint of softness
   break the surface like a rippling shadow then it
   sinks again

185
I've been looking at the sky as though I too were
   a sky

186

two guards standing with metal gadgets in their
   hands
begin to search me
going beep-beep at my metal belt buckle
and at the silver of my cigarette pack, beep-beep
lifting my legs one at a time
he checks my soles
and I slide through and at last come to my bunk
lie down and think about you baby, my bitch, my
   puta, my clown-girl,
my woman, my Mariposa, my friend
and I think how I hand each of these women-
   selves in you
prune them with my love or let them fly wild in
   heat for me,
healing me with love.


187

Sitting here, a foot in front of my head is a fence
then a slender corridor where the guards walk
then another fence, then a space where men
   sleep
then window with gray and rusty bars
then a thick wall, then outside pebbles, treeless
   dirt,
then a granite slab of thirty-foot wall
and barbed wire, then behind the barbed wire,
   sunglassed guards
pace like clocks, tic-toc, back and forth
always ready to trigger the last minute of a life
that rings with too much freedom.

\*

194

You're with me Mariposa and I'm feeling like a
   million
because we are together, we stand in line
   together
and get shook down with the electronic wand
   searching for shanks
we get shook down about five times a day,
   coming and going
and you were with me when the guard runs his
   hand down my legs
under my belt and you and me smile cuz he
   doesn't even know
you're here and you sticking your tongue at him
and make funny faces, you were with me today

195

Now my Mariposa, I am going to lie back in the
   night
under my night lamp and read your moon
   talking poem,
and fly to you, over fields I haven't seen in five
   years
and streets sprinkled with lamps of nodding
   light
and turtle small cars in distances crawling long
   lonely night roads
and I'll listen to the wind
and go sniffing here and there and take large
   strides
your way, through tingly night air

passing over sleepy blue rivers
slightly above hordes of night crowds and
    flashing neon signs
and keep moving over mountains brushing my
    hands
along their different leaves and tree lines
over closed shopping centers and state houses
and long deserted streets and small cafes and
    trucks on the highways
over cows in pastures and fences and ranch
    houses
pass through spring showers and over happy
    frogs splashing below
over telephone wires and cables and gaunt steel
    structures
and now smelling dust mingled with sea salt
now heavier green smells and the moon closer
    now
and now see deer below, a few stray dogs
    grappling for homes in alleys
see there a stranger walking down a ditch
and the black swamp water glimmering sparkles
and pass over dark homes one window full of
    light
and I keep flying, keep coming
until I sense your breath along my neck
and I reach out for your arms
and without a second gone I enfold you
belly, legs, hair
as your hands begin rubbing warming me
and I whisper Mariposa, aqui soy tu hombre, to
    Colibri

196
Oh, people, I am in prison but do not give me
    sympathy
I sit here watching the dusk and dreaming of
    love.

197
It's Saturday morning here, some of the men
are up at the cage rapping with the guard,
some writing letters home, some lying
on their bunks, awake, thinking on small things
that in prison loom large as ever, the rest
sleep because there is nothing else to do.

198
I have picked the seeds out of my rotting life

199
the greatest wisdom is found in darkness

## December Nights

The sky like black paper
drying in desert heat after the rain,
and this prison sitting like a run-down shack,
on the outskirts of everything,
where people stop only when they must.

I reached up a long time ago, and tore
that black paper away from the sky,
and saw the clear stars like dimes scattered
on my bunk after an armed robbery:
I keep hitting the heavens when it's dark
with a 45 magnum dream, and someday I'll hit
    it big,
blast the moon wide open, and on the other
    side,
just sitting there, will be freedom.

## This Voice Within Me

This voice within me waits in line,
and after my anger and laughter go to sleep,
it is earliest to awake,
and stands in front like a peasant
in a bread line, or a bearded bard
at a slum soup kitchen.

I open my eyes on the gray and snowy world,
still drowsed in darkness and dreaming,
and I see him down there all alone,
and call to him, accompany me,
listening to the sounds of waking life
around us, I smile softly at my cellmate.

## LOOKING

I feel something in me
move—
one movement in particular
crawls out of the dark in me,
a dead hand on bloody drugged knuckles
unfolding,
coming to life.

To hold in its palm,
lines of my heart's untouched essence,
and the callousness I wear,
when nothing else will light
my path,
or marry them, two separate ones to me.

# Excerpt from Letter to Will Inman, 5 May 1977

There are mountainous regions we have yet to
  map out within
our voices, the themes . . . are sometimes great
  signs
pointing the way . . . they are not domesticated—
they are tribal songs to be shared by all . . . no
  one
can keep them for themselves. because humanity
spins through them, not individually but as a
whole nation/tribe lofted up or ground down to
fine powder in the wind, water, fire and earth,
the poems are signs that tell us things. if we
place them side by side, we see they point to a
direction. they have broken from the circle of
today's petrification in the cities and have left a
gaping hole in the fence. if they patch the hole
up so none of the slaves will get ideas about free-
dom, trust that i will be behind there to barrel
thru again. and i am not afraid of the hunting
parties and passels of critics that will tag at my
heels. we can lose them easy enough. but they
will be blind in our world. . . .

# FROM
## SWORDS OF
## DARKNESS

# The Young Men Are Laughing

This morning, by the wall, laughing.
I stand ten feet away from them, listening,
  looking
out in the undisturbed street.
  Willy the wild man will open his pawn shop
    soon.
There's Red skipping down the steps, looking
  for a fix.
Wizard bums a smoke from Nacho, and calls to
  Delon for another smoke.
The men all laugh. Voices go back and forth: Ese
  bato / Eh Tommy /
    Danny comes down with a bag of banana
      cake.
Wizard's working out a deal, saying, "I'll pay half
  now
and half later." Wedo calls to Chuck, ain't no
  more cake.
And big John whistles at a woman passing.
  Sunlight pours into the streets. A few cars
ride low, pass slow. Deals are made for Sunday
  night, on the corner.
Someone whistles. The men all laugh.

A man up at the window yells, We're trying
to sleep up here chumps! Pay no mind. Big John
   says pass me
your cup. A little whiskey goes around.
        Say man, C'mere man. John, let me av piece
dat cake, says Charles Ray. Everybody's talking.
   Their shirtless
trunks, shirts slung over one shoulder, in the
   sun.
A trash-can top cracks the human voices on the
   street. Dogs and
cats. And Charlie moved back, just around the
   corner, did you
know?
        Old songs drone from windows. Beenie got
           ten years.
What you say you gonna do, man? What's the
   story, man! Say Tiny
we ain't got no electricity / eh! Against the wall,
   the men laugh.
        Saturday morning. Some will move out of
           this
neighborhood today, some will move in, where
   the Health Dept.
blurbs our water has to be purified, and Flaco
   got his tape deck
ripped off, and Big Blue turns to a Christian
   after dusting two cops,
and Whale couldn't go to his pop's funeral
   because his sister
stole his money, and Rose in Polock's eye is a
   young sweet boy

of twenty-one that just moved in.
    The only Eagles flying here are tattooed on
      arms.
And old black Dean dawns his pure starch-white
    porter's uniform
and dignified, walks to work around the
    boozed-up sidewalk gangs.

                         Aug. 27, 1977

# A Desire

Out of the barbwire, the walls, the timeless days,
a desire forms in me, alongside my heart like a
 rock:
I stood with both feet squared and firm on the
 ground,
a ground made of rock, and I pounded that
 rock, until,
from the blast of my Will Power, a sliver of rock
sank into my heart, going deeper and deeper
 and deeper,
and no matter how I move, still, I cannot evade
 the pain of my weakness.

A desire is in me, as strong as any rock, as sharp
 as any:
it was the wall's hard hands, the barbwire's sharp
 nerve,
and Time's cruel endurance, all working in
 hand,
the pumice of a death, refining it, molding it,
and when I slept, it rose furiously from within
 me,
my flesh the hilt of its blade
that went down in me, so far, this silver root

of a new beginning; my tongue a steaming hot
   petal
in the cold new morning.

A desire heavy with furious flames throwing its
   dark shadow
on the lightness of life,
and all life seemed a glass window, and a flame
   there,
breathing against the thick glass,
churning its painful flames against the glass,
against flames against each other,
churning out shadows in creamy waves,
the cold wind avoiding the flames, beneath my
   eyes,
beneath my eyes were the flames and I filled
   with shadow.

The desire, the flame, pulled at the night;
the sleepy-skinned, soft and warm space of night
it drew into its sprawling glow of fingers.
And the night falling into its fiery palm,
untangling from contours of stars and moon,
ripped from the sky filling the fire
with a fragrance of it being all there was, all
   powerful—
my destiny, my only care. This pulsing desire
for new life, new ways of thinking, of seeing my
   humans,
unleashed a love-freedom in me, a freedom so
   free,
it took apart all I was, and put me together,
into all that I was not.

# I Turn My Little Fan On

Air blows across my face.
I could be in any number of places.
I could be any number of people.
Air blows across my face.
Eyelids on my tawny face, flecked with sweat,
closed, half moons, unburned and tender,
my eyelids down now, as I rest my eyes,
seated here, on a summer morning, in a cell.

I awoke early enough to see the sun
spearhead through the bars,
ooze over tier screens, a ritual paint
smeared on a humble hut of mud:
biblical blood on my door of steel.
A plague ferments in the air,
violence, insanity, treachery.

Lord God, I'd like to call to you now.

Silence, my Guardian Angel,

you step over the fallen mindless bodies,
their souls and hearts
thorns on barbwire that tangle up your wings.

Silence, you are like a wild animal
caught in a trap. When I first approached you,
you snarled with pearly teeth of pain,
your wings bristled,
your husky yellowed claws flared.
Nonetheless, I came forward and set you free.
I thought we would go our separate ways,
but when midnight sets in,
I hear you scratching on the closed door
of my heart. I open it.
You have become my family.
Through the torn sleeves of my soul
you lick my wounds.

Air blows across my face. I open my eyes,
look out my cage door at the heavy faces.
I could pick out a million places
where I'd like to be now. I could be anyone,
anywhere. Air blows across my face. I am on
the beach at Corpus Christi.
It is a nice day.

Lord God, I'd like to call on your hand now.

# WALKING DOWN TO TOWN AND BACK

Along dry slabs and pebbles,
hot rasping birds and broken shrubs,
the lazy shuffling horses
parchly munching leaves,
their hooves in soft malt dust;
lubberly, nothing disturbs
this sun clobbered land.

Walking to Belen, past dry clay
crumbling river banks, over
a cracked tar highway, no longer used,
and in the same with the railroad tracks,
buried in weeds and sand.

My father used to kill the bulls here.
A lot of children would catch blood
gushing from the neck, and drink it.
We wanted to be as big as our fathers,
big shouldered, big hearted,
with arms strong to hold a cow down
or wrestle it by the thick brawny neck.

Walking now, in the sun . . . that was eighty-nine
    years ago.

There is a bar here now. A few Indians and
    Chicanos,
the same people, different tribes, shoot pool and
    laugh.
I don't know how, but we have endured.
In the mirror my sun-burned face, wrinkled now,
wonders how we endured. I wipe my lips,
and offer my glass for another fill-up.

Hours later, when evening rolls down the
    Sandias,
a black stallion rolling in red dust,
and water is pungent with alfalfa in the air,
I stand for a moment and smell, thinking of
    fields,
outside the bar, the sky dark blue.

Walking home, I smell wood burning
    somewhere.
My heart kicks like a young calf at the hot iron
    brand
of memories, my frightened eyes and black singe
    of old days,
marked on my heart, belonging to them.

I was wild as canyon water then, just a boy,
smoking marijuana under an old capsized
    wagon.
My father came by on his horse, "Let's go!" he
    hollered.
I didn't want to go, I was waiting for a friend,
to go to a dance. My father reached down,
pulled me up with one arm,

threw me behind him on the saddle, and off we
    went!
We rode out to an old woman's house
who had seen Our Virgin Mary.
Her husband had died, and back from the
    funeral,
thousands of snakes converged upon her house.
Baking in the front yard, as soon as she opened
her door, they all swiveled alive toward her.
For three days, until exhausted and off guard,
she fell asleep: when the snakes, in one writhing
    heap,
began creaking open the bolted door,
their odious smell, their slimy swishing of bodies,
twining around each other making a big dark
    ball,
wriggling at the opened crack.
The windows were black with crawling snakes,
small speckles of sunlight between their clotted
    undulating.
She took her dresses, all the wooden furniture,
anything that would burn and she piled them
    up—

    the door burst open!
With a stick from the fireplace she lit her
    belongings,
the mass of snakes fell to the floor, scattering in
    clusters,
twisting themselves in the flames, their mouths
    flared,
        the flames engulfing them!

But through the acrid smell and black curling
	burning snakes,
came others, their tails in flames, their swaying
	heads in
flicking vicious agony, closing over flaming
	snakes,
blackening burning weeds, or grapes stomped
	underfoot,
oozed insides, red pink and bloody, burning
	bright slosh—

	she threw a clay pot of gunpowder in!

Bits and pieces of snake splattered on the wall,
over her face, smooth, grainy blasted rippings,
rattles, seethes, and sighs in the glare of
	explosion,
a violent wrenching of bodies battering the wall,

	and then a settled silence.

In the stink and putrid slime and squirming
	death coughs,
from a point in the middle of the smoke,
dilated a growing light, a bluish growing edge,
overpowering; then silence, and Our Virgin
	Mary in the smoke,
light green surrounding Her.
She gently floated in light out the broken door.

	When we got there,
about fifty people were huddled in prayer.

My father jumped off the horse, quickly knelt in
the hot dirt,
and began to mumble prayers with the sign of
the cross.
I ran over to the water tank below the windmill
and drank water.
People were singing and weeping in the huddle
of bent heads.
I sat under a tree, angry because I couldn't go to
the dance.

I went to sleep smelling the sweaty horse,
and hearing mumbling prayers in the hot sun.
My hands up to my throat, I could hardly
breathe;
when I awoke, pins of light straight through my
eyes,
through my breast to the very core of my heart!
Clumsily trying to get up one knee,
I saw as I clutched my breast, Our Virgin
Mary . . .
the horse spooked and reared away galloping,
I shaded my eyes, and finally on two trembling
legs,
followed Her to where the people were
gathered.
The people cried out when they saw the light
around me,
"A miracle! A miracle!"

I see the burned charred house now on my way
home,
the water tank empty and eaten away with rust.

In the moonlight, on his horse, I see my father,
coming after me, and a snake moves through
    the brush
at my boot . . . on my way home each night.
People come out here to get away from the city.
They drink in their cars and pickups out here,
and when I pass only a shadow by them,
they hear me talking and think I am a drunk.

# RUDE

Life is so rude to me. Leaves my head
spinning like a hurled lid of a grease can,
wwwwoooorrrrinngggg to a stop on cement;
creaked-up wood my bones, as it drives its green
  vines in me,
carves another year on me,
     battered  by life like a rug at its front door:
     its heavy foot too quick, slides,
     and life lands on me, breaking a leg.
     I am shook out, hung on a line of tree
      boughs,
     and there ants and butterflies crawl over me,
     spiders usurp my knots and twines
     with silken nest for dew and eggs.

All this, living among drug addicts and blood,
among bottles of whiskey splintered in streets,
trashcans upended by black children playing
  warriors;
     Life is rude, rude as a knifeblade.
Life is a cord dangling with a death charge
while it sprays out light and sparks,
     this cord plugged into us, taped up with drugs
     and money wrapped around it,

clamped by laws, silver shining laws;
we are all electricians,
looking for the short in the line,
tearing out our walls and insulation.

I have often seen that certain glow
in a man's eye,
and rings of energy flow from a woman's
   hand
into mine, often that glow
is what we call endurance and love,
is why we do what we can't understand;

that glow is the sea where our treasures come to
   rest,
spilling out the gold coins and gems,
as the green tongues of our dreams shoot out
like a frog's in the grass bottom of sea,
swallowing the wingless treasures buried in sand
   of the past.

Life is rude, is that rude guest we hope
will never appear in our homes,
knocking like a stranger for a piece of
   bread,
stranger blown in by winds and snow,
traveling across America on an empty belly,
the one you hope will never come to your
   door,
looking in your eyes, without a word
telling you the truth of what you long tried
   to hide.

                              Sept. 26, 1977

# FROM
## WHAT'S
## HAPPENING

## What's Happening

At this moment, fires of a riot are everywhere.
The men call into the smoke, We Want Justice!
Eyes blear from smoke.
In a cellblock the size of a moderate community
    church,
fifty, sixty fires are spewing everywhere.
My eyes are crying . . .
the water is turned off, the air conditioner off,
a sandwich for lunch, no breakfast, no supper,
the men scream, We Want Justice!
And this morning a Mexican is shot to death,
two weeks ago another Mexican was critically
    shot,
and the Black gangs are locked down,
the Chicanos and Whites are locked down,
and fires burn and burn before each cell,
voices scream and scream, We Want Justice!

The entire prison population quits working
in fields for three cents an hour,
in the factories for a dime an hour,
and fires engulf the tiers,
illuminate cell after cell
long deep eyes stare from.

Behind the flames and arms cloaked in smoke
is the cry, We Want Justice!
My cell fills with smoke, I can't see anyone or
    breathe,
and six hundred men cry, We Want Justice!
The fire! The fire! And men cry out, Strike!
Viva La Huelga! La Huelga!

Music is playing above the flames, above the
    smoke,
and I am weeping with my hands over my face!
My cell fills with more smoke! I can't see the
    bars!
The whole cellblock is a huge billow of smoke!
Over the floor sewage reeks ankle high! Urine
    and feces!
Everywhere, flooding, and the water is turned
    off,
garbage piled up for weeks catches flames high!
    High!
Smoke and more smoke and more smoke!

No one can see anymore, but hear the raging
    cries,
Viva La Huelga! We Want Justice!
Men are screaming in their cells, behind the
    bars,
behind the smoke, flames and weeping, Men . . .
we live like this . . . this is rehabilitation!
Grotesque Murderers! Ignorance! Waste and
    Blood!
Beatings! Robbery of Dignity! Sickness of Soul!

And through the smoke men's voices call,
how you doing over there? You ok?
And some yell, play the song I like, I love!
Play the one about the man that lost his woman!
About the one that fights for his freedom!
Through the smoke! The fire! The Murderers!
  Play! Play!
Let my soul feel once more the shudder of those
  days!
When I was free and human! Let me hear it and
  weep!
And the songs play, and the men sing along,
old sad faces and voices alive in the fire,
in the smoke and bars in their cells, they sing!


From far away in the night, you can see the big
  cellblock,
a sparking mountain of rock, jutting up, higher
than the mainyard walls, up, with six hundred
  men in it,
you can see the square windows filled red with
  fire,
from the flues on top of the roof shoot sparkles,
sprouts gray smoke,
at the windows red against the night flames
  jump,
pouring flames through broken windows,
expelling black gray smoke,
in the night surrounded with blackness,
and inside in the fire and smoke,
in foot deep sewage, are the cries, We Want
  Justice!
Viva La Huelga!

And the weeping, and the hate, and the blood!
And the despair, and rehabilitation!

Inside this furnace are the men, human beings,
  voices crying,
screaming and eyes weeping!
Poor Whites, poor Blacks, poor Chicanos, poor
  Indians,
who yell, turn the water on!
Let us flush our toilets! Let us drink some water!
They bang against the bars, shuddering rows of
  steel cages!
They bang against steel bars with broomsticks!
In the midst of flames and music and blood,
in shit and grime and smoke and scars and new
  wounds,
they scream, turn the water on!

And I am weeping! I am sick!
I have had enough, and yet every day I go on,
while this poem is read aloud by someone,
I am going on, and the sky is filling with black
  smoke,
the windows are filled with flames,
and I weep! My eyes burn! My lungs are black
  with smoke!

# I Applied for the Board

. . . a flight of fancy and breath of fresh air
Is worth all the declines in the world.
It was funny though when I strode into the
   Board
And presented myself before the Council
With my shaggy-haired satchel, awiry
With ends of shoestrings and guitar strings
Holding it together, brimming with poems.

I was ready for my first grand, eloquent,
Booming reading of a few of my poems—
When the soft, surprised eyes
Of the chairman looked at me and said no.

And his two colleagues sitting on each side of him,
Peered at me through bluemetal eyes like rifle scopes,
And I like a deer in the forest heard the fresh,
Crisp twig break under my cautious feet,
As they surrounded me with quiet questions,
Closing in with grim sour looks, until I heard
The final shot burst from their mouths
That I had not made it, and felt the warm blood
Gush forth in my breast, partly from the wound,
And partly from the joy that it was over.

# STEEL DOORS OF PRISON

The big compound gates close the world off,
Lock with a thunderous thud and clunk,
While bits of dust scatter into your lungs,
Breathing in the first stark glance
Of prison cell blocks behind the great wall,
Breathing in the emptiness, the darkness

As you walk with an easy step on the cold
    sidewalk.
Then another door locks behind you.
This door is your cell door. A set of bars,
Paint scraped, still as cobras in gray skins,
Wrapping around your heart little by little:
The ones you love cannot be touched,
Christmas, Easter, Valentine's Day, Mother's Day,
All seen from these bars, celebrated
With a deep laboring yearning within,
While the cobras slowly wind and choke
Your mind, your heart, your spirit,
You hear nothing but the steel jaws close,
Slowly swallowing you . . .

# OVERCROWDING

The maintenance man was banging loudly
Fixing the mechanism above one of the cell
    doors.
Showers were sputtering out water on each tier,
TV and radio sounding deafeningly in a duel
All over the cavernous cellblocks extra loud,
The last of the cons just returning from supper
When they found Gary lying up on the tier,
With stab wounds too numerous to count,
"Looked like Swiss cheese," one guard said.

I caught a glimpse of him . . .
Face covered with a sheet, one blood-spotted
    boot
Dangling out of the sheet,
One puffed and pale hand turning blue,
Being wheeled out on a stretcher.

The same night, clearly from my cell,
I could see a tremendous fire engulf a cell,
Flames lick upward ten, twenty feet in the air,
Bulging out from the cell,
Thrusting outward past the wire screen
That runs along the tier,

Flames gurgitating, throwing a yellow glow
Into the pitch black cellblock,
To the far end of the cellblock.

Last night a fellow picked up a steel pipe
And beat his cell mate with it.
The bludgeoned one appealed for help
With horrid fear-stricken jittery cries,
Screaming out for the guards for two hours,
Until finally one arrived from Arabia,
Glum eyelids and a sorry about that ole bud
But I was having my coffee.

Prison is a dead man's zone.
Looking into the eyes of men here,
There is something more than cautiousness,
A sense of complete cold barren knowledge,
Of being abused too long and too far,
Coerced into indignities that pile up on them,
Into conditions that make them reckless and
    savage,
Watching the Directors of Prisons on TV
Fiddle with lies, sliding past the truth
That really exists here, the impending
    violence . . .
Turning around and around us daily
Like a gigantic snake slowly choking us,
Sinking its fangs as the poison seeps deep
Day to day in this Arena of Death,
Where hope seeps through the cracks of our
    dark skulls,
And lights go on to start another day,
As if nothing at all had happened last night.

# AH RAIN!

Sweet scented, dripping from eaves and
  darkening
plastered walls.
Muggy air! Goblet heavy and dark goldfish
filled with rain!
In the forehead of my brow is thunder!
My heart orange-colored,
my body an orange grove dripping with rain
and pungent with acids and roots, dead leaves,
thunder! thunder! thunder! in my forehead
lighting my darkened grove, shook branches
and petal dripping and bough snapping,
soft earth I plunge seeds to like sword tips,
in the crackle of sky my soul is,
in the sweeping winds, I lift my head high,
expand my chest to breathe! breathe! breathe!
breathe in the wood and green leaves,
in the musty earth, the rotten compositions
that create in their rot such famished beauty,
sweet and thick with life, dunked heavy
in rain, to swirl in our mouths life, life, life.
Body that I am, bone hard, black handed babe,
heart that I am, crushed raging aflame timber,
soul that I am, a hard chicken-pen dirt,

rain seeds, spitting down seeds,
the sun claws like a morning rooster.
The rain, rain, the rain, I put my head down,
so humble before my master Rain,
I drench my body, shimmer, clothes wet,
my religion is Rain, my anger, hate, love is Rain

# THE RUSTING SKY

And the red hours dripping from its mouth
into the belly of blackened cities.
   A light haze circles the city, a bluish red
like inside a cathedral, where widows come to
   pray
for long dead husbands.
   I play possum in my sleep after dinner.
I know all the time night is surrounding me, I
   can't look.
Not until a human voice wakes me, or a cry from
   the street
calls me, or a door opens and I know a friend is
   in the house.
But to open my eyes only for the night? No no,
   it's too strong.
   So strong that all the shadows rising from
creaky buildings, and growing out of our hands
   and bodies,
so strong is night, that no shadow can protect
   me from its
brightness.
   What brightness, you may ask? One that
      glasses

my soul, so to move would break it. A brightness
that hurts
these eyes on distant childhood days.
        And still darker the night grows. Only trees
survive the night. While cities smolder from after
work tiredness,
and we are drowned in hot stuff of our hearts,
and buttons
are loosened, straps unstrapped, and odors of
our homes
smell like a wolves' den, kindly the moon drops,
calming
shapes and forces of our souls.
        The night! the night! the night! The half
of me rising out of me, sinking into you like a
leg, that
kicks up at the stars, and hangs lazily over the
horizon,
as if into a river that none dare cross but the
dead.
        My life slows down at night, unwinds, taut
muscles of the mind let loose their grip on
weights, dropped
in a dusty moll of dust at my boot heels. And the
looseness
I become, filled with brightness now, like a bag
of light
I punch at, that hangs from the sky! I am
punched at by trees,
by winds, swaying and babbling thuds. And the
night turns darker.
        Until there is only night. And I know I am
weak.

There are mascara'd gas stations in bright red
 signs and orange
eyelids blinking off and on. There are old
 houses withered up
like shriveled plants in their lots. There are dots
 of light
that nail the dark. The night spins with great
 revolutionaries
and hoodlums, with the loving and maddening.
 Like a cyclone that's come to rest in our
  hands,
that tomorrow will whirr out from our veins, and
 glaze our eyes
with a blistering veil. Yes, but tonight we tease it,
 for we
own it. It sleeps, this strange power that makes
 us who we
are. We slide from its presence sleeping at our
 feet like a cat,
or a small child, and out the door we go, or
 indoors we come,
with a different mind and heart.
 And the night sleeps, darker it gets. But ever
calm, as though knowing our destinies, it sleeps,
 sealed
in a separate world; I almost touch, and can hear
 and feel
it almost.

# I Think of Little People

       Who tomorrow will be twenty-one, who now
fly on swings, kick at playground dust, and in
   cool sand
tunnel their tiny fingers to imagined dungeons
   and hidden
bedrooms in a forest, next to a pond, collared
   and coated
with flowers, shining bright its love.
       The sneeze of bone-racked pipes amuse
          them
late at night. And cubby holes loom as large as
   caverns.
The grumbles of bricks, the squeak of stairs, all
   hold such
a castled cacophony, their tiny souls bloom,
   blossom out,
from each creak, and grumble and sneeze.

       This enchantment they tuck in twenty folds
like a special coin, laid in cloth. And they take
   the one
remaining year, and slash through the jungled
   field,

slowly, clearing a plot, cutting their fingers,
   aching their bones,
looking to the sky, and to the eyes of a woman or
   man.

   Small humble children now in the
      playground,
   on the merry-go-round,
   on the grass,
   and beneath trees by the ditch, where water
      runs,
   in your caps and different shirts,
   your messy hair and great great cries:
   any of you, it's told, could lead the world
   to be a better world.

I come here then, and stand awhile, looking on,
   to learn from you.

   Your mothers and fathers lounge tiredly on
      grass.
   And they are beautiful, the men
      outstretched
   on the grass, and the women glancing time
      to time,
   to the children, and beyond to something
      beyond.
   Cars circle the park, small birds in trees
   turn a quick brown eye down to their noisy
      radios.
   The shade has a mossy velvetness here,
   across the carpet of green bright grass.

Ah, children children children, I love you so
    much.
And to you grown-ups in this semi-garden, to you
the holy fire of this poem is intended, to bring
    again
that coin into the light, upon our palms,
If only for a moment, then replace it in the folds
    ourselves are,
and relax upon the grass, shade passing your
    faces,
and then sunlight

*From*
# Rockbook 3

## WE PRISONERS

With keys in our hearts,
keys so worn and rubbed,
waiting for a hand
to open those empty rooms.

## My Heart

A hungry river basin,
at the wind's edge,

my desires sleep
like hot sunstones,

until the rain
awakes them.

## Your Letter Slips Through the Opening in My Heart

Pressing the darkness out,
like a sudden lamp in a room,
diffusing the walls and pictures,
all the furniture of my memories:

I pause home again: you are not here.
I pick warm left over words from your letter,
like last crumbs scraped from the dinner table,
place them in a tattered cloth
and fold it in my coat pocket.

I turn and close the paper, shut the envelope,
and walk down a dark hallway,
past sleeping rooms and down endless stairs,
until my feet pause, and I stand staring at your
    address.

## The Distance We've Arrived At

I've lost touch
with the green woods
in the last . . . the last,
what do you call years so empty?

Only "them" and I a "thing" to you,
who's lost touch,
and we both dream our own seasons,
our own fields beyond walls.

## Living My Other Life
*for Norm Moser*

Sleeping when I heard the mail arrive.
I hoped it would be you,
then from behind my eyelids
scolded myself not to hope.

It was you. You told about
the 57 chevy breaking down again,
about you working long hours,
and the cops arrested Alfonso again,
and laundry on the clothes line,

    and my cheek feels the warm wind of the
      barrio,
    your bronze legs curling out and down
    from the hem of your dress
    to the floorboard, we're going to your tia's
      house,
    my body wants you . . .

and I put the letter down,
place the pillow over my head,
continue to dream of us.

Emerging from darkness, your face,
your lips stimulating my name,
and your body curved, bending its stem
in a sensuous offer of budding desires,
my flesh crowd like fire on,
my arms around you like flames,
swept and torn like a sail
washed upon brown sand shores. . . .

The letter and the envelope
chilled and stiff, but comfortable
to my hand, like a warm body
sliding between cool sheets
late at night. I shivery slightly,
thankful and tired; I unfold the page
and into my palm falls a green leaf,
a green leaf searching a palm,
a palm a secret meaningful touch,
I lift the leaf between my fingers,
touching it with a questioning silence,
accepting our meeting, and not wishing
for the park, the long walks with you,
your words flutter up to me,
and entangle themselves on briars
of my heart, grown wild with desire
behind these walls.

# Just Before Dawn

Mumbling bootheels of guards
crush as if fresh snow down the tiers,
grinding silence crackles like icicles;
the blood dreams mercury heavy
as the flashlight swings into each cell
in thin white scissors counting heads,

while spiders, cockroaches and crickets
scurry across the path of wary guards
whose bootheels tip tap down dark tiers,
while sparrows stir in the black rafters
and cats slink into the cellblock from the cold,

morning breaks over old veterans of the
    wilderness,
hair white as morning frost,
their closed eyelids footprints
of a wounded animal in the snow;

And young prisoners hug their blankets
like frozen carcasses strewn across
timeless blizzard plains, and a few
gnaw their hearts off
caught in the steel jaws of prison.

# Dreaming About Freedom

What I would be doing if I were out,
what kind of things would surround me, and
the people I would talk with, and touch.
It's been a long time, a woman's hair,
her breasts, the singing of her touch,
or crawling around the floor with children,
all take their place among the stars,
among Capricorn, the Twins and Venus.

I think I would probably go out at night,
and breathe the fresh air, listen to the tinkles
of town glitter in the night, I would probably
    pause
by lawns, knowing how they understand
me, with their aromas, and flush out my wild
beautiful thoughts and feelings, like wild birds
so easily scared away by the sound of closing
    cages.

# QUETZAL FEATHERS

Lying down on a bed, dying,
with old fingers he places quetzal feathers
on his ancient gray head,
then entering flowing green forest of his
   thoughts,
he drums untamed air,
whips faster the feathers,
shreds silence with this long gliding flight,
descends into thick viney treetops,
and downward into wooded trails,
among other birds
where he met the sun's eyes behind each leaf,
and offered to the sun his feathers,
then entered the heart of the sun,
like a bird in the sky
forever disappearing into the sun,
with a smile on his already pale lips.

## SATURDAY

freckled leaves after the rain,
water pools sprinkled like paw prints
over the streets,
    with bare feet
    my heart dips
    into the rainbow
    by the red cloud.
as my dog
shakes water from his fur,
I shiver with wild joy!

## Things Unexplained
*for Norm Moser*

Lowering her eyes
lowering her eyes again
again. . . . . . .
how can one explain the sensation of touching
    this?
by a word? Well . . .
until I do
it will fall away, ferment, the picker will miss this
    fruit
the earth will take this fruit
as breath from my soul
and eat it
it will bring beauty to her arms and legs
perfume for her winds
and someday when a small breeze is blowing
under my nostrils
I'll catch a whiff of this beauty
that originated from me
and from behind the blindfold of life
I'll peek
how she lowered her eyes
lowering her eyes again
I'll write.

# SILVER WATER TOWER

I remember when I was a child,
on weekends my father and I
drove down to visit my grandmother.
We took the old road, and my father
smelled like part of the land,
and as we came closer,
his face took on a wholesome expression,
and it seemed the history of the land
shone bright in his brown eyes.

I looked to his face, then out the window,
and saw the first sign of my little town,
where my grandmother lived,
and the silver water tower stood
on tall lank steel legs;
ESTANCIA, boldly lettered black
across its silver tank top.
It was by the school where my uncle worked
as janitor,
and by tall green grass he watered,
and I played in when a young boy.

It was the sign that home was near,
where the link of my true blood was unbroken,

and thrived solidly in a little silver hair'd woman,
with ancient customs, y pura sangre nuestra;
a home my father became son, y Hombre,
and I a wonderful miracle,
un Nino, another generation, de mi raza!

It was here where I found myself,
with time to sit outside in the shade,
and talk of chili, cows, trees and horses,
time to walk through fields to a friend's house,
time to understand the meaning
de la familia, de la raza, juntos,
luchando para abanzar, el foturo destino.

Like so many Chicanos, in need of work,
driven to the city from their way of life,
I rebelled, no con mi mente,
pero con mi Corazon,
and I came to prison.

I am not allowed to lay on the grass here;
it's Saturday here, I lean against the fence,
my back to the prison water tower,
still, I feel joy, me siento a toda madre,
about coming home again.

# With My Massive Soul I Open

With my massive soul I open
my brother's heart,
where fire rumbles,
rocks grind against each other,
and the moon rots in wounds
of black branches across his eyes.
In the fire base metals of my voice
unswirl molten,
on the dark as light,
whether sword or figurine of brotherhood,
the mold awaits in him.

The compliant pretty face, the soft padded
   shoulders,
of Integrity, in soft soled shoes of a sycophant,
in pantomimic cities, chemically lifted to climax,
with gold boned laughter in their hearts,
while despair flaps over the land of sybarites,
whose lives crumb for crumb, grain for grain,
root for root,
are in the service of banks.

       America,
I look at you with distraught eyes, I,

stroked by storm's smoking hand, I,
among untampered, temperamental young wild
    winds,
that give their soft hair and young bodies,
to trees and flowers driven mad,
placed in even lines,
I, like twenty mule teams
lugging boulders across earth, up mountains,
evaluate you,
I, a wind at your furrows,
I, rain at your furrows, destroy the symmetry,
and discern new cultivation,
feed seeds of what I see and feel,
with dreams, a new reality.

I want Justice afoot in each house,
whether parquet floor or mud floor.
I do not want its sweet face,
its drop of blood pinched from a pimple,
or a cherry in a gentleman's evening drink its
    pride.
It roars at a culture's silence
by dropping its judgment, a great avalanche of
    rocks
upon the guilty breast, and polished boots get
    dusty,
dark roads where robbers feast, close down.
But today Justice does not do this.
I want Justice to be a beast free of reins,
    unrepressed,
respected over the earth.
I want it here in America, while we sit before our
    fires,

to approach out of the shadows we fear.
I want its raw bellow
to awake our lethargic hearts like a sleepless
   whip!

But in dark valleys where cities thrive,
Justice leans against a lamp post,
lips painted pink, or in private clubs,
panting under red lights, she fingers g-strings,
while patrons count their money.

I know she does not need this,
and does not need million dollar lawyers,
she needs us,
and here in this cell, I take
her chilled calloused fingers in mine,
brush gray hair from her old faded eyes,
and with my shaggy spirit around her
for a warm blanket,
I watch her drink the bitter medicine of my
   struggle,

Medicine found in the heart,
in the common needs of common people,
medicine made with my hands and eyes,
medicine made from hunger and lies and
   violence,
medicine of the blood of each living person.

# A Handful of Earth, That Is All I Am

You drive up to my shack. Unclip your briefcase,
    on the hood of your new car
spread a few official papers, point with
  manicured fingers,
    telling me what I must do.
I lift a handful of earth by your polished shoe,
    and tell you, it carries the ways of my life.
My blood runs through this land,
    like water thrashing out of mountain walls,
bursting, sending the eagle from its nest,
    that glides over huddled seeds as do my
      hands.

I carry wisemen in me, I carry women and
  children in me.
    beneath my serape I put my hands to warm
      them in the morning,
and build fires in the night,
    that reflect swords and flowers in my eyes.

My heart is a root in wet earth.
    You tell me you are not to blame for the way
      things are.

Invisible fingers wrench my life away, plunging
   deep,
      carrying a handful of wet earth.
Mountains give me their patience and
   endurance
      when my children look up to me.

They ask me, Oye Papa, how can a skinny man
   like that
      take away our land?

The earth filled with my tears and blood!
      But my wife knows
my arm is twisted behind my back,
      tearing the joints, a boot crushing my spine,
my lips to the wet earth, whispering to her,
      I shall speak no lies
and cry only truth to my tormentors.

I look into the man's face for a long time
      when he tells me there is no other way.
Then stare at his car as he leaves
      and carry his image in my heart
that he is blind too,
      and speak with him there long after he has
         left.

## TAPESTRY OF DOWNTOWN

The grumbling charred factory.
Its stack a black bone flute,
mournful songs of smoke
wheezed by withered lungs
and fingers chapped as desert brush,
scrawl across the unscrubbed sky
dull gray notes of hope,
puffs of sand in our eyes.

On one of the old factory windowsills,
six birds have made their nest,
huddle their shale feathers
against the sharp cold of morning,
bundled up, dark barbs of coal.

Twitters crack like dry twigs,
kindling crackling in the icy dawn.

The first spark of sunlight
catches the windowsill,
their wings ignite, flurry,
brown flames tossing in the air. . . .

## Black Mare

On the white rocky driveway
her steel shoes clokk clokk
softly against white painted rocks,
nostrils spew steam,
her chest fills with dawn,
her large head dips to nibble,
newly sprouted tufts of grass
between white rocks,
at a daisy she shakes her mane
Black Mare! Black Mare!

# NEW DAY

In dark
Sharp enough to cut your throat,
A thin moon
Edges steadily on, a glass cutter,
Across night sky,
Brushing, blowing into piles of clouds,
Little slivers of stars
That settle in sleeping hearts;
Until, in the little break,
Twilight starts twitching with life,
So happy, it melts the moon,
In its warm dawn,
And aches our hearts that just awake
from starry dreams.

*FROM*
SET THIS BOOK
ON FIRE!

# PART 1

# In '78

It was prison, rioting
for our rights, burning mattresses, pounding
steel doors an inch thick,
slate, steel-painted-industrial-gray years,
fat-jowled, gut-butting, thug guards
who waddled on stumpy legs to our isolation
   cells
swinging batons, spraying mace, beating us
KGB fashion.

# I've Taken Risks

starting as a kid
when I stole choir uniforms
from an Episcopalian church
so I'd have something to keep me warm that
   winter.
I looked like a Biblical prophet
striding in six layers of robes through dark
   streets.

When you turned up the ace,
you kissed the card. And when the joker scoffed
   at you,
you were led away by authorities.
Second chances were for punks,
two-bit, jive-timing, nickel-diming
chumps.

It was beautiful in a way,
to see us kids at seven and eight
years old
standing before purple-faced authorities
screaming at us to ask forgiveness, muttering
how irresponsible we were, how impudent and
   defiant.

That same night
in the dark all alone, we wept in our blankets
for someone to love, to take care of us,
but we never asked for second chances.

# I'VE SEEN TOO MANY

prison catwalks with guards
cradling rifles, monitoring me,
to trust anyone, too many
barb-wired walls
to believe what people say,
looked in too many mirrors,
at too many photos
of friends and family
who died early and violently,
to believe what you say.

Understand:
all I have to be grateful for
is my little fan in summer,
my pills on the small table
where the second TV sits
with bent rabbit ears,
my empty Coors and Bud
cardboard boxes
I carry dirty laundry in
on wash day,
that window in my room

that allows me to look
out on hard streets
and dream
for a better life.

# THIS DARK SIDE

has always haunted me,
fiercely adamant in its opposition
to all the good I create:
subversive and defiant.
While my spirit revels in light,
it
gorges on cesspool pleasures
leaving my spirit at times a fly
and maggot-infested carcass, dissembling
my dreamwork, disintegrating it back to sand
wind scatters, blows
back into my face
I have to lower in shame.

Imagine a ladder of light, a trellis of branches
rising out of my soul in blossoming radiance,
carving its own latticed speech in the sky
toward the sun.
Imagine
my dark side freeing the termites to gnaw
down these branches.
My soul
falls like a black oak tree cracked by an ice
    storm.

It stares up with a skull's nightmare grimace
of cruel suffering on its frozen face.
But hovering at dawn,
hope like a butterfly floats around it,
a powdery rainbow dust effusing the air
with pervasive peace.
And then
the morning yawns forth like whispering lilac
on the air.
My heart untangles itself from its dreams
like wild honeysuckle grandly striding into halls
   of sunlight,
trickling with dew beads of grace
that sigh from my lips.
Some power moves in me,
a divine dancer elegantly celebrating its
   existence.

I tell you now,
the dark side arrives unannounced
with cold hands,
scoffing at my efforts to live a single day in
   dignity,
undermining the goodness in me,
though I'm getting better at exposing it,
standing before it like a brittle twig
smashed under its wrecking tank tread.

All that I've despised and spat at in disgust
I've become at certain moments in life,
but I continue to praise the spirit,
refuse to embrace the utter horror
of self-destructive impulses.

I draw the curtains of my life shut,
a silent stranger to myself
chewing on the maddening, shredded remnants
 of my heart.
Accepting it as part of me, loving it,
not afraid of feeling its pain, understanding
how I always contradict myself,
I succumb to passion,
even indifference,
roar my loss and abandonment,
bell-bellow my cathedral soul,
trust and suspect
in a constant flight between light and dark.

It never ends. This harsh beauty,
this struggle not to retreat in fear
but to celebrate what's hard earned, staying true
 to myself,
is what it's all about.

## Let Me Give You a Portrait

not as pretty as uniformed La Crosse players
on an expanse of grass
in one of those
passion-drained, Ivy League schools,
a portrait
achingly real as chipped, rotted
teeth in a hobo's mouth:
direct your eyes to the peeling
picture of Saint Nino de Atocha,
that child saint who sits on a throne
with a hat with the brim turned up,
holding a staff in his left hand,
an empty reed basket in his right,
two vases of flowers before him, smiling cherubs
above circling his sacred face.
He's the one I've put through hell,
when most of my friends left,
when my boss fired me and my landlord threw
    me out,
when I ran out of gas one hundred miles from
    El Paso
and I caught my girlfriend screwing that joker,
when all I had was an opened pack of stale
    crackers

and dead cockroaches in the cupboard,
a jug of cold water in the icebox
for my father and brother's hangover.
Santo Nino de Atocha was there
thumb-tacked to the wall
water-stained drab green, with a medal of Our
    Virgin Mother
hanging over the faded retablo from a nail,
    veiled in blue
with hands folded, face pleading
with God to accompany this crazy boy
roaming the night streets, stealing and fighting,
and doing so I believe because
I had a pure heart, long before prison and
    county jail cells,
before drugs and whiskey and guns came into
    my life.
The pure heart I carried in me
was like a simmering volcano mouth
where roses grew and rocks talked,
where fire was my light on the hard journey,
where the journey work was staying true
to the dreams I believed in as a kid
when I folded my hands and prayed
kneeling at my cot, believing in miracles,
that angels were swirling around my shoulders,
that my dead uncles and family were present in
    spirit,
that no matter where I was at,
jail or streets or some forsaken, roadside motel
    room,
Santo Nino de Atocha accompanied me,
held my hand, guided me away from harm,

and was the reason why
the bullet missed me,
the cops ran out of breath chasing me,
I got cigarettes in the *hole* in jail,
I didn't get hurt in a fight,
I found ten bucks on the sidewalk,
I read my first volume of poetry.

# I Put On My Jacket

Wrapped up, I went out in winter light
climbing in volcanic rock on the west mesa
feeling softer and meaning than I've felt in
    years.
Amid arid scrub-brush and bone-
biting cold, I thought of Half-Moon Bay,
how the ocean unscrolls on shore
with indecipherable messages.

Only those hiding out
from tormentors and tyrants, those in jail,
gypsies and outlaws, could understand.
The ocean talks to me
as one prisoner taps a spoon to another
through four feet of concrete
isolation-cell wall.

# I Have Roads in Me

winding within my arteries
into distant hills
of memories,
where dreams float like dandelion fibers
on bright, chill, breezy
mornings under a canopy
of cottonwood branches.

Where leaves glimmer
sunlight
roads turn.

I have roads in me
where drums pound a sacrifice
and beckon
to again believe in life's wonder,
where I learn the intense passion,
seeing the sparkling, dewdripping
leaves upon moist, pine-needled ground.

My heart restored,
I am guided
by stars
and a raging desire to live.

# COMMITMENT

A county jail guard knocked out a tooth
smacking me across the face with his club once.
I took that tooth and sharpened it on my cell
    floor
to an arrowhead I tied to my toothbrush with
    floss
to stab him with it. I never did,
but with the same commitment, I once took my
    brogan
and a cot-leg of angle iron
hammering it against the bars to escape, which
    I did.
Hammering that metal leg for months,
I finally cut that bar they said was impossible
to cut through
with a boot and cot-leg.
It's a lesson that if I can do that,
when it comes to the business of living,
I can do anything.

# PART 2

# In '88

I married Beatrice,
who bore two angelic children
with hearts glistening like gold
beneath a clear, snow-melt, mountain stream.
We grew together on Black Mesa
encircled in a pool of magic light,
rippling rings of Saturn light effusing our
    happiness,
her laughter wild as a foal testing its legs
galloping through high alfalfa, scattering
yellow and blue blossoms in its wake,
her presence in the house
a warm refuge.

## SUNDAY PRAYER

O Great Creator, I thank You
for watching over my children
and their mother, for keeping their beauty safe
and for guiding them through
all life's perilous journeys.

Give my children strength
to improve on
who they've worked so hard to be.
Gabriel's just stepping out in the world,
twelve years old and leaping high
to catch stars; clip them to his heels
like spurs as he rides his Cannondale.
Antonio seems like he's willing
to grind his feet in earth
to make his passage honorable.
I thank you for them both,
their winged spirits gentle and compassionate.

Dear Lord, keep me straight
on my path, don't let me veer.
Love me, bless me as You have,
let no harm come to my house.
Let this day be a good one,

prime the deep roots of my being
allowing them to bellow out into blossoms.
Give me the willingness to live decently,
to be a man whose acts match his words,
to think before I act, to love before I hate,
to see before my eyes are closed.

## The Reason I Wake This Morning

is because those people who've lived
through tragedies and loneliness and anxiety
found in their shattered-pottery hearts
fragments that fit perfectly
into the puzzle of night stars,
into the joyous cry
of a child at dawn
dashing out on the playground,
into the hands of men like me
who rise and dress and walk
out the door, culling from winter light
residues of summer
to dream a bit more
of the growing season.

## Celebrate

Five hundred and five years
tortillas slapping between mamas' hands,
farmers irrigating red and green chili, squash,
   and corn rows,
forming halves into wholes, braiding
two roots into one thriving, ever-deepening,
   mother-root
bridge between black and white,
blood rainbowing
opposite shores,
connecting south to north, east to west.

Five hundred and five years
of prayers mumbled from lips,
hands clasping other hands to endure,
keeping the line intact,
unbroken hope, rosaried faith,
from Incas, Moctezuma, Cortes, Villa y Chavez,
to the anonymous men sitting on park benches
meditating on the dawn,
to women climbing cathedral steps to attend
   Mass,
to whimpering, wakening infants
suckling at their mothers' breasts.

Five hundred and five years
and still they remain
all beating with strong hearts,
strong
hearts celebrating the magic songs,
acts of courage that leap from them
and integrity
that shines from them.

# In the Foothills

of the Sangre de Cristo Mountains,
the land undulates into mound swellings and
   unfolding flatness
the moon seems to nest in,
settling
into scrub-brush, parched-arroyo runoffs
where as a child I believed
if we hurried we'd catch the moon,
touch the moon—it was just over the next hill:
   *Another hill, Mama! Hurry, Papa!*
   *We can still catch it!*

In the chase, my being emerged renewed,
a prairie hatchling,
to later stretch its wings and struggle free
birthing into innumerable multitudes of men,
nest within nest,
abandoning one to make another,
migrating toward seasons of laughter,
caresses, anger, troubles, joy,
and friendship.

## GRANDMA

And when they come, as they have,
I seek strength in your humble memory.
As contrary and farfetched as my metaphors
and images may seem,
to a woman
in the hot, dry prairie,
when you walked, I knew
somewhere in the world a great pianist was
   playing
to your steps.

O dear sweet ancient woman
who never uttered a word of complaint on her
   behalf,
when you looked at beans, corn, squash,
a simple glass of water,
your gaze held a melody of a hundred choirs
singing in harmony,
all in unison
thanking the Great Creator
for our many blessings.

I remember a woman who was
sometimes mean and cross with me,

who chased and shooed me from the house on
    wash day,
who made me scrub my face with freezing cold
    water.
Your faults were cliff-edge fingerholds
for anyone brave enough to climb to the summit
where sights could be seen only angels were
    given.
I climbed there many times,
and as many you called me your angel.

Today, when I'm besieged by enemies,
when the easy way out haunts me,
when I'd prefer to sit in a cantina and drink with
    friends,
when doing drugs to forget the pain of living,
when I struggle to live with dignity,
when I promise to try harder,
when all my vows of conviction turn syrupy,
when the blood drains from my lips,
I kiss your face again in memory
and tell you to watch me, just watch.

I will not surrender
to the worst part of myself, Grandma.
I will be a man you can be proud of,
one who has learned well from you.
And when they come, as they do,
I'll wade out into the fields,
parting weeds, ignoring briars,
flying all these flags, hollering:
    *Your weapons mean nothing to me,*
    *I have Grandma in my heart!*

## At Lori's House in Wisconsin

We peer into the foliage
weaving the north side of the wall,
pushing aside the tapestry of vines and tendril
  braidings
to view inside the robin's nest for an egg
concealed from sight.
        *I've seen her,*
        *but she hasn't been back in a while,* Lori says.

The mantle of mutinous leaves and stems
is a reflection of the blazing passion of spring.
I want to keep my heart that way,
recalling a wistful sentiment
of past innocence.

So many changes happen when we fall in love.
Our days are filled with passions, supplicating
  our lover
for more love, more,
and as years pass the vine leaves
of our well-gardened soul chill
like beggars' rusty-edged cups
rattling against deserted-street curbs.

I toss crumbs to sparrows beneath the apple tree,
thinking of
the great concrete and iron baseball stadium in
   Wisconsin,
how Lori and her family took Gabe and me
to see the Brewers play,
a magical evening
of uniform composition,
from the white-chalked lines, to umpires, to
   players' uniforms,
to the broad vista of infield and outfield clipped
   grass
beautiful as a bride and groom before the
   preacher taking vows,
the scoreboard, cheers and moans of the crowd,
hotdog hawkers and beer caterers,
me imagining
Little League kids whacking that ball,
skittering around bases—
game days
that'll never be forgotten,
just as acrobatic marvels on the monkey bars and
   swingsets
or that first time upturned in a canoe at the lake,
fun times
that transcend all our adult worries and broken
   pledges,
experiences that tune our souls
to a poetry humming, hound-howling our lives
at the moon;
how our lives fill the empty nest of each day,

brim it with mottled-egg dreams of our naive
  childhood
that ripen our lips like long-ago first kisses,
reddening as the years gray and wither,
and aged twigs begin to fall from the nest.

# It's an Easy Morning

In the overcast sky, in those clouds
that hang over the Sandia Mountains,
a sax blows notes like raindrippings
from pine needles, darkening boulders
reminiscent of medieval churches
with worn tapestries, shimmering blue
glass altar objects, feathery
designs in the altar stonework,
making me think of loves I've lost,
loves who committed suicide—
in solemn procession through my memories
cloaked parishioners under hypnosis
carrying broken hearts to outside grottos
where the Virgin Mary smiles
out on field birds
and livestock sluggishly wakening at dawn.
I praise short lives, and believe
their souls blend into the gray
Rio Grande, coursing between broad,
hefty cottonwoods that crowd the banks,
emptying into the ocean
where I hear them whisper
when I walk the beach,
what my expectations are,

asking if I've changed,
do I believe in God,
ebbs and tides of their voices
irreplaceably etched in my bones,
exhorting me to write
as real as the sand my feet print.

## Sometimes I Long for the Sweet Madness

The mystery that would spiral
my soul into a seashell
some seafaring explorer
would blow in his coming,
his arrival, his company,
his joy, his discovery.

I carry myself out in winter light
hoping music of any kind finds me,
leads me into its song,
just a note scored on paper
some child somewhere
in some faraway country
cries out at sunrise.

# I Move Through

the day in a fog, realizing
unless my fingers touch something
I'm lost. Unless I pick up a scent of coffee
or my eye catches the honeysuckle tendril
  blossom
swaying softly by the outside gate, my life
rattles hollow and haltingly.
I'm used to
passionate engagement, not this boredom.
Even my dog has slowed; how he used to
wander, thrashing out fowl from fields,
barking robustly, blue flames spiraling
from his ears and short tail:
he's a bird dog in a rabbit world,
and his age is starting to show in his lazy,
closing eyelids, in the way he muses
whether he should rise when I come out
with his food. Could it be this suburb we live in?
We both count the days when we can move again
by the river, well up in the mountains,
away from all this order and structure,
to piss freely in the yard, to lay back on rocks
and stare at the stars, caressing stones
as if they were a lover's hair.

# I Am Uneasy

this morning,
my heart a radar disc assaulted by strange
blips and beeps from quiet suburban streets
and cleansed, law-abiding citizens.
Even their dogs are shampooed and combed,
which I don't criticize
since mine are grungy, mean-eyed,
  bore-tempered,
claw-tusked mongrels
who don't give a shit at midnight: barking curs.
I suppose like me they feel ill at ease
with this altar-boy life.

One of the many defects I have
is I chew my fingernails, chewed to the cuticles,
snubbed-and-clipped, blunt buns
I nibble and yank at
unable to resist the morsel of torn flesh
or sharp fragment of fingernail,
spitting a piece out of the window,
tapping the steering wheel with bloody fingers
as I drive into the crazy city

acting like a trained, bill-paying citizen
when I'm really a bandit wanting to blow up
the Gas, Electric, and Telephone Company
buildings.

# THE FIRST HARD COLD RAIN

came battering
over the west mesa dunes and black volcanic
    rocks,
west from Gallup clattering the decrepit
shag-steer corrals. The sound of
bailing wire whipping windows
in the suburbs woke me,
and I want to thank the Lord for this
miserable morning, beautiful
in its dark raging, staining
mock-adobe, stucco-suburban two-stories
where lights in windows flick on
and responsible parents rise
to breakfast and work.

I've been anything but responsible,
neglecting laws, cursing authority,
jeering meatless, ham-bone statesmen,
spewing my gangland rhetoric
cloaked in a smile
for cookie-jar enticements
and dinner bells ringing beans,
chili, and tortillas, but that's not what makes
this morning so miserable.

You see, after the smoking,
teenaged, snub-nosed days cool,
and I find myself
comfortable in my destruction
and shortfall of accomplished goals,

the serpentine, blue-scaled rain snaps
the screen door and pops chimney tin,
shimmering streets I look out on through my
    window
in t-shirt and underwear. Memories
of old friends sharing Tokay wine
in Texas barns on alfalfa bales
come back to me, or traveling
in that beat-up car
when sunrise over Big Bend cliffs
made me believe in miracles
big as Texas. Realize:
I don't need to be what you expected I should
    be,
nor apologize for my cat-burglarizing days
or my raccoon-pilfering-dog-food-
from-the-bowl-on-the-porch ways. Realize:

on dark, rainy mornings like this, men like me
are nothing more than birds in a fruit tree
they tried to chase away.
But we got to bite the ripest fruit first,
spoiled the farmer's weekend at the grower's
    market
when he had to explain to customers about
    them damn birds

that got his fruit, trying everything to keep us
  away
from gorging on life. We
who refused to be caged canaries
didn't mind getting our feathers wet
just to feel what it might be like
to fly into the storm.

Storm-ravaged, that's the image I was looking for
when I said goodbye to my son this morning
as he was leaving for school,
my youngest still asleep in bed, when I made
  space
for my children to start their journey.

I don't mind this miserable, cold rain
so beautiful in its discomfort,
its sweet ravage familiar to me
from those steel-toed, heel-rocking,
bloody-knuckle years when I rode
at night through the Sandia Mountains
whurrumphing my Harley, gatling-gunned back,
throttling for a taste of real life,
to fly like a bird. Call it art,
antisocial. I call it love.

# PART 3

# In '98

How all the beauty
ended up out
on the garden trellis
like an unused fishing net,
my dreams rusting, red tricycles
in backyard weeds,
dry-docked old boats on bricks,
stray dogs chasing cars
that keep getting hit.

# GHOST READING IN SACRAMENTO

For days I feel a ghost
trailing me, memories aching and joyous,
from kitchen to basketball courts
to walking paths to driving around town,
a presence hovers about me
like the incipient, tight-furled rosebud
on the verge of breaking free, and I realize
miracles come in colors, soft bruises—
the mean scowl of a drunk
in a corner booth in a bar,
the elation a kid feels freed
of morning chores, leaping and running
out to the playground. I feel startled,
surrounded by memories,
like one of those sailors who finally comes
  ashore
to kneel before a humble altar, surrendering to
  feelings
that the world is too large for him to see it all, a
  man
whose heart once radiated stamina, strength,
  and firmness
yet now like a sail is folded to the mast:
from Charlie whirling in old songs

mimicking oldies but goodies
to Gilbert's miner's grubbing for gold
in his coal-shaft past
to your solitary dance
in a room filled with dreams
to David's hunting through jungles of cells
tracking a cure for AIDS
to that guy in Sacramento
who made us all realize something more beyond
    ourselves,
who drew our thinking out of our eyes
in tears, his voice a sudden catching,
kindling and flame,
reminding us of our own flickering journey.

# THE TRUTH BE KNOWN

I quit writing to study cooking,
to learn how to make a delicious tortilla,
to devote my time to creating magnificent
   gardens,
fragrant, enchanting patios for friends
designed with the moon and stars in mind.

Down at the San Jose Community Center,
I shoulder a satchel brimming with poems
I've composed to teach kids how to read and
   write.
I buy them pizza and soda,
to make writing a pleasurable experience,
associate it with food, friendship, and laughter.

The next morning I wander store aisles,
reading book spines, searching for poetry
to give to adults pursuing their GEDs,
but the poetry either lionizes the poet
as a savior of Mexicans
crossing the border
or makes the images so exotic
it compares the ordinary fork and spoon

with dormant volcanoes,
losing my attention in the process.

We need a shoe to be a shoe,
for the poet to describe the foot
inside, the miles walked, the weariness
that seeps into toes, heel, and calf,
the tired dreams those feet lug every day.

I return to my abandoned cabin,
become a wild man
dancing Irish jigs to nature,
babbling nonsensical Yeats rhymes to myself.

# Poets Can Still Have a Good Heart

and have a past riddled with violence,
a strong heart and have known addiction,
a good heart and have known drunks and
   thieves.
Do this: stand
before a group of Uppidees,
admit you know someone with AIDS,
someone in prison,
someone homeless,
someone with mental illness,
someone handicapped.
It means
while most turn away their hearts
you face life, use the sweet impulse of pulsing
   blood
to live your life,
not to live a lie.

I'm in the garden this morning
pleased the roses are so bountiful,
awed by the lilac's treasure of fragrance,
honeysuckle vines flourishing,
climbing over each other up the wall
toward sunrays, shivering with hungry freedom

for the open-road radiance.
I don't remember my dreams this morning
but keep a journal next to my bed in case I do.
Its empty pages welcome images, voices
sifted and tunneled through my waiting pen.
I intend
to compose poems
of friends who died in recent years.
I keep talking to them, hearing them in my
   head,
admirable acquaintances I wish to honor,
ones who stood, who labored against oppression
with heels dug in dirt against retreat:
voices, brilliant comets
subverting the dark.

# It Makes Sense to Me Now

That evening
I drove down from San Francisco to Los Angeles
and dropped in to visit Luis,
who told me:
    *It's your turn to carry the torch.*

Years later
the significance of those words
flared like a stick-match in the dark
the day Paz gave me a painting
of Nahuatl Dancers
tethered by the ankles, who fly
around the pole.
The lead Dancer, El Maestro, stands on top:
he's back from visiting the sun,
bearing a message for us on earth.

At dawn
I make my way downstairs
to make coffee, nodding
my respects to El Maestro:
bunches of flowers on his hat,
yellow/red/green/blue headband tassels
ribbon out in wind.

He beats a small drum and blows his flute,
a single eagle flaps by clouds behind him
as he balances on the pole;
the reddening, orange-gold sky ablaze
with light.
I wonder what his message is
and how it pertains to me.

Now
I drive twice a week to San Jose barrio
volunteering to teach reading and writing,
and I remember

one evening
I asked the children and parents to write a letter
    poem
describing their journey to America:
risking lives, homes burned, fleeing death
    squads
after husbands and brothers were murdered,
the women raped. I'll never forget

when
this little girl, too shy to read aloud
her praise and love for her mother,
had me sit on the floor next to her
as she stood on a makeshift stage
in a bookstore. When she uttered that first word
a glint of light sparked across her brown eyes
into the world, as if it were golden
speech without sound. I sat amazed
at the light in her eyes, igniting a memory in
    me—

when
I too recited my first poem. The intensity and
   radiance of
a child reaffirmed my original reason for writing,
one I'd forgotten along the way.

Suddenly
I knew, keeping the light intact,
not teaching writing, not to mold or direct,
just to keep it burning, blowing on the embers
so hope doesn't go out,
that was the message El Maestro was bringing me
from the sun.

# I Wish My Life

fit the day's needs
as coal in winter or ice in summer. You never
  know
when you're signing for your happiness
you're not signing your execution papers.
More incredible's
how folks use faith in God
to ignore the starving, to be
indifferent to the homeless, assume
God will punish those who locked the boxcar
suffocating those Mexicans locked inside
like the human beings who rot in prison.

I'm called spic, wetback, illegal alien
because there is a god.
And if I get paid what I've earned, deserve for
  honest labor,
another law is drafted to keep me a slave
while preferential treatment and advantage are
  given
to the rich calling the shots.

I don't mean to be insolent, to sound pontifical,
but I know

nonsense
when I hear it.
Instance:
at UNIversities
where professors are more Uppidee
than a stretch of snowy Kansas field,
rarely do they trust Chicanos or Indios to teach,
only those with rug-burned knees.
Instance:
Governor of Arizona, found GUILTY of a slew of
    felonies,
airs his grief before a press conference, quoting
from the Bible
how prophets are often considered lepers in
    their own town.
Now come on, I'm thinking,
this is getting too strange.

Were I to speak out
on the absurdities
like Jordan making more in five-second sound
    bites
for NIKE
than thousands of rank-and-file workers in a
    year,
I'd be glared down, accused of race baiting,
diagnosed a danger to myself, committed
to the unspoken
BLACK LIST.

I've heard gibberish
from friends living in gorgeous coastal homes,
driving deluxe Beamers,

the bark and arf-arf of their buried-bone bits of
  beliefs:
> *You're a danger to yourself.*
> *Ask the Holy Spirit to heal you.*
> *God is free, independent of all nations,*
>   *not funded by the state, not subject to king.*
But when I ask them for donations to buy books
for disadvantaged children, they reply:
> *I give my gift basket at Christmas*
> *through the church.*
I guess there's room for all kinds in this life.

## The Journey Has Always Been

what we didn't do or did, how far we've come
to a place
where dream fragments smolder:
hot pebbles cooling after a summer rain.

It happens I am a singer of the heart
and took my songs to the gutter to sing them to
    drunks,
recite them to addicts,
whisper them to thieves and madmen,
outstretch them like my hands
clasping prisoner's hands
through cell bars.

You see, it's these people who understand the
    poem's magic,
who are not invited into society,
whose opinions we denigrate as useless,
but each unlike Uppidees fight hard for their
    existence,
battle against armed keepers to speak, stand,
    and breathe.

They've known the blessing light of the poem
on their trampled hearts,
the poem's respite in a merciless society,
its sensory indulgence in their own severe
　　deprivations,
its love and respect
away from the mockery, ridicule, and shame
that accusers heap on them.

The poem's words
scrub away the rust on their hearts
drawing out the burnished luster of their
　　dreams,
and radiates a certain light from their bones.
As they roam the murky alleys,
it transforms their suffering into songs of
　　celebration,
strengthening their convictions
to stay when ordered out.

Commanded to sit, they stand.
Asked to speak, they withdraw into silence.
They are, in other words,
true to the poem,
loyal to the heart,
merging the two.

# My Dog Barks

Come close, listen: at the door a professor from
   Flagstaff asks
can I participate in a conference on prison
   writing.
I decline. Conferences are squeamish about
   truth.
If your words don't fit their theories,
if you claim that convicts are people,
that writing goes deep in the soul, to memories,
to flesh and blood, that writing has more to do
with cruel guards and torture chambers,
   isolation cells
and chained beatings, they become squeamish.

I know a man
in Paterson, New Jersey; the guy
wasn't allowed to write a letter
to his wife after she had their child,
so he hid himself away and wrote
a poem in blood.

I visited the house where Thoreau lived once,
where he wrote of the oppressed and murdered
   in prison,

how they're imprisoned because they're poor,
how they have human rights. He wrote
about humanity, not just about writing
as with those whose work seems detached
from their own hearts, not like the conference
    types
who believe there is no way to help
the imprisoned, that it's best to keep them in
while having workshops on prison writing.

I talk back, think individually;
this is strictly a conference on writing
in prison, and if you had writers who'd been
    cons
it would make the conference a success.
But you don't want to hear what they're going
    through,
you prefer to translate their suffering into MFA
    papers,
to turn their deaths into metaphors,
to make their real cries and real terror a tone in
    the text
that people outside can philosophize about;
it's only about writing, not what would free these
    men
from their tormentors. Besides, if they weren't in
    prison
you wouldn't be able to have a conference,
    would you?

Come close, listen: I decline the offer
to pander to suspicions,
decline not to discuss what drives the writing,

what the writing really means,
what it means to be a writer in prison in the first
    place,
not some yahooing convict with a book
whose fame is built on kissing ass.
And while I'm at it, I decline your myth of
    censorship,
where every bookstore in the city prints
handouts about some food in Podunk or New
    York
burning a book: that's not censorship, that's
    bullshit!

The writing conference definition of censorship
will hail the work of some gawkish clown
who's never been behind bars—portray him as a
    victim.
Or take that girl born into uppercrust, tsst-tsst
murmurings. After doing a book on the border,
right away she's a heroine of the underclass,
jailed entirely for symbolic purposes.
O how they offer their wrists to the cop!

Come close, listen: the real definition of
    censorship
is when they keep you locked in the *hole*
for ninety days without light or exercise
so you have to compose your poems in your
    head
and remember them. The real definition
of a prison writing program
is when a prisoner has to write
a poem in blood.

# ANOTHER POET I'VE KNOWN

This woman I honor, respect, am blessed to have
   as friend,
who picked me up at O'Hare Airport in
   Chicago,
who'd been through everything
unimaginable, enduring it,
growing like a blueberry tree, more leafy
grace in her gestures, her rotund
laughter, heady
with mysterious gaiety in her eyes.
Raped once by four policemen,
her man murdered by the FBI,
she retreated
into deep, green mountains with her daughter
to retrieve
that crystalline innocence
of the dewdrop in her tears,
to douse the flames of her agony.

Yes, I've known a woman
who took me from Chicago to Milwaukee, who I
   thanked
for picking me up,

who drove three hours late at night, renting a
   new truck
because her car was too old and might break
   down,
who worked ten times harder than any tenured
   professor
while getting paid half her worth, half
what her male counterparts made.
I remember her at the table
with students of every race, color,
seeing how they respected her, how she lavished
attention on them.
Not one award,
no plaque of distinction, not one NEA
grant adorning her walls, a commoner
of the sort who make the real world habitable.

Her spirit splendor mists my loneliness,
the kind of luminosity I see hovering
at the river's banks, burning away at sunrise
disclosing landscaped fields, bright streams,
   mountains.
She was that for me, this poet living
in her small apartment with her doves,
   parakeets, and plants,
Christmas lights nailed above the kitchen
   doorway,
rising early to make tortillas for students, guests,
creating cards to send to friends
splendid and elaborate as Diego Rivera, collages
sprouting in her hands like seeds
in soil moist as farmers' field rows.

Blessed I am
to have known this woman, blessed
I am to be her friend, this angel
who said of her life:
    *It's a Chicago thing.*

Frida Kahlo's brow, her eyes,
lush hair, sensual hips and breasts.
Paintings hang in every room,
stations of the cross she recorded
on her journey
from hell to the mountain peak,
cherished faces of the people she loved
in the center of her bleeding heart.
I'm awed by her healing, like magic
that deep, raucous laughter bordering each day,
her life a pine forest
abundant with eagles, fragile creeks,
a solace to weary travelers like me.

Just a woman,
mother, painter, and teacher,
another poet I've known.

# With Paz By the Fire Last Night

We talk about the warrior's journey
when suddenly he looks up, and says:
    *It's the rage I have trouble with.*
I wake and have my coffee, write,
go to the mesas to walk in canyons.

I admire the layered clouds, winter light in sage,
find a campsite littered with shotgun-shell
    casings,
plastic bottles and canisters riddled with
    buckshot
an outlaw hangout for gun lovers.
I cut and floor the pedal
bouncing out on the dirt road
and see a couple walking their dog,
realizing how life keeps reminding me
I'm doing what I should be.

A phone call from a woman needing help,
a reading by an ex-con who memorized my
    *Crying Poem,*
a small speech I gave for the New York premiere of
a new documentary on adult literacy,
a benefit for Leonard Peltier's defense fund,

a meeting with Fortune Society members
to talk about making it on the streets—
the soul is what matters, how drugs infest the soul
with diseased, cancerous muck
that must be scraped away, cleaned off with prayer,
the sheer work of living healthy.

Tutoring barrio families to read and write,
volunteering my services with joy,
always rushed and exhausted, I move into winter
   light
that invigorates my resilience
to endure the betrayals of haughty, Ivory Tower
intellectuals, academics with all that
musky ineffectualness hunkered down in
   booklined offices
trading the classroom in for festivals in the park.

I cry into the mike for commitment,
avoiding journalists, TV reporters, interviews or
   articles;
calling Guadalupe in the mountains
to deliver wood to impoverished families
whose only source of heat is fire.
At dawn I tread rocky trails
breathing in cold air, absorbed
in the phosphorescent brilliance
of dew and cold on sage stems.

The winter light remains
a written testimony on my journey
to clouds and light and shadows
always moving, rearranging, rushing

into canyon crevices.
The phone is ringing, the letters stack up,
bills need to be paid, my children attended,
a novel and various manuscripts edited.

Sensitive friends drop by with booze and drugs
to shock to life their own dead systems.
I note the signs every day
that I'm moving forth
alone into winter light,
into a place where flowers grow in snow
and tears are made in flames.

Looking back on a broken marriage
and substance abuse, I see it as a time
when locusts swarmed across my heart
eating away the nurturing marrow of green life
and leaving a wake of dust-bowl bleakness,
a shadow of a man holding his brimmed hat on
   his head
fiercely leaning into howling gusts,
roadless, mapless, stung and pelleted,
a shriveled, gaunt, life-starved skeleton,
each day's casket closed, submerged in oblivion.

I find myself meandering a coastline
observing the gulls ride waves gracefully,
shimmery feathers tucked into their sides;
in the distance fog wraps mountain peaks
and coves quell in peaceful slumber;
my footfalls leave deep imprints in moist sand
where I see tides sucked in and vanish.
I imagine grief goes that way,

that change comes like the ebb,
a playground teeter-totter
or windblown, child's swing at dusk.

The wind rides the swings,
lifts and drops the teeter-totter.
Amid screaming divorcees
and lung-cancer patients,
a lone gull alights on a log
left after the flood
that hurled refrigerators a mile downstream,
backfilled rooms to ceilings with mud,
juggled and tossed entire homes
to smithereens against cliff banks.

I see how fragile plants endure,
how they bulk with weighty blossoms,
and I understand the beauty of gulls
in winter light, riding cold waves,
taking no provisions for their journey,
no map or army or money,
no crude baggage from the past.

They dive into a blue, ethereal reef-world
and the sea caresses them
like a loving hand behind a dog's ear,
who shakes awake and barks to go outside
where dewy frost burns off in sunlight
that warms the bones of travelers,
who long ago lost their dreams and now have
    only stories
of loneliness and love, danger and courage,
to tell around the fire beneath the stars.

# SET THIS BOOK ON FIRE!

Rising
in the glow of the embers,
and even in the ashes, I want to tell you:
I've spent years
studying stark cries in the cancerous marrow
of inner-city streets. I've gone to
Uppidee districts to witness poets
who kiss their asses while adjusting grins,
luring audience approval with politically correct
    quips.

I want to tell you:
don't lie! If you're going to read a poem
about a kid getting his head blown off,
don't raw jaw your cotton-tipped tongue
to gain the sugary aplomb and donut favor
of English Department heads, who like you
and never scavenged food from dumpsters, who
    like you
and never stood in welfare lines, who like you
while gleaning misery topics from *The New York
    Times*.

I want to tell you:
if you're going to preach what you don't follow,
testify to what you haven't lived,
hoola-hoop your way like a pride-plucked hen
doormatting your heart for moneyed admirers
whose concerned faces ooh and ahh faked
    empathy,
know that poetry deserves better than that
hee-hawing, educated, hillbilly-mule
whinnying for the crowd response.

I want to tell you:
while you do your sheepish, poor-me routine,
your victim-in-distress sighing,
poor people are being murdered,
prisoners are being zapped with fifty thousand
    volts
of electricity to make them behave.
O hollow-hearted, New Age activist that you are,
tell us in your poetry how coolly you've risked
your life helping refugees cross the border.

I want to tell you:
what you're looking for is a new title to acclaim,
what you want is to be hailed a savior
when you spice your poetry with theatrics,
crumpling on the floor and groaning with rage.
O how the world has done you wrong!
The last thing we need is more toothless tigers
stalking thousand-dollar checks from
    sympathetic patrons
of first-class airlines and four-star hotels.

I want to tell you:
I'm weary of these castrated Uppidees,
poets and patrons who've hardly engaged in life.
I'm tired of the prejudice they never own,
tired of them spouting off familiar remedies
to a world of ills they've never known.
I beg you both, get out of the way,
please step aside, just a couple of steps,
it takes too much effort to go around you.

I want to tell you:
the flashpoint of paper is 451 degrees.

# WHY AND WHEN AND HOW

did our lives move from the page
words composed so elegantly
boy's choirs could harmonize,
how did they scatter
like crumbs on the floor
swept up
and tossed from our lives
to decompose with the rest,
how did our pastoral
move from the canvas
to join the mob in madness
when we dreamed we heard angels
whisper once in our sleep?

## RITA FALLING FROM THE SKY

Because of the drugs they gave me
that damaged my brain
I have been unable to speak for myself,
but now that it is over, and I roam the hills
of my village again,
    I will try
        to tell you what happened.

When I was born my Creator said,
"I will put this stone that fits in my palm
under this water,
and in a hundred years, the water falling on it
will chisel out a hold, and through that hole
you will see the secrets of my creation."

I, Rita, who fell from the sky,
am the stone, carrying water and onions,
and I walk alone,
across deserts,
borders, and across lands of many cultures,
I follow the water
        dripping on my soul.

They say it is a mystery
that I did so, that I survived.
I am eighty-two years old,
and despite what they believe
I know where I come from and where I am
     going.
I lick my lips so much
because I learned from the snake to taste, to
     sense, smell
danger and intruders with my tongue,
also because I am thirsty for truth, for love,
for my land, my people's lost songs and dances.

Enough destruction,
enough talking.
Enough greed/violence/lies/betrayals.

I walk a world created ages ago,
a world where I killed my husband
because the horny toad spoke to me,
the goat and the llama
urged me, and I still exist,
and for penance I walk thousands of miles
across desert and prairie
across international borders
with only onions and water,
onions and water.

How, the doctors ask, did I do it?
they wonder, make up stories,
call me insane.

I have told no one
what I have seen, who I am now,
how I have changed,
the marvels
I have encountered,
the friendly spirits I have met and who gave
   me
their blessings and wisdom.

But the doctors think I am crazy
and I let them believe I am mad,
but I will tell you the story, who I am,
why I went,
what I did—

My name is Rita from the Sky
and what you have done to me is not fair.
I escaped the State Mental Hospital in Kansas
   twice
because I heard my ancestors calling me.
What you have done to me God will punish.
I leave when I hear the ancestors speak to me
they whisper
      to me in the nopal cactus
      in the exquisite
      prairie blossoms and the sage and the
         prairie doves.
Have you seen, I want to ask,
a prairie dove?
at dawn, plump, they veer here and there,
carousing with the dawn light,
as if they are aware of angels

in every flower, in every rock, in every
tree.
They are like my heart feels, that's how they fly,
at dawn,
how my heart feels for humanity, for my people,
the sorrow, joy, the sadness that is so great
that nobody even knows.
     Instead they say I am mad,
and I walk, walk, and walk
back and forth in my cell,
thousands of miles, four steps one way, four
     back,
thousands of miles.

To keep an old woman in this cell is mad,
but I cannot contain your madness,
the insanity that sane people have,
     tearing up the forest, killing the land,
dirtying the waters.
     I hear prairie doves singing to me
in the rocks and sand and dirt and sage and
     cedar and mesquite
I hear their wings as voices
telling me there is a sacred religion
that none of us are aware of
but which I hear.
I hear the singers singing words that make me
     feel
alive, make me feel part of life, make me feel
as if my heart means something, makes me feel
I am a woman, and my journey means
     something.

I am telling you what I am about, what I am
    made of,
what I hear and feel and how I live.
I hear those singers in the grass, in each of
    my footsteps,
in my breathing
I hear my ancestors
Mayan kings,
my Toltec ancestors
praising my skin color, praising my strength,
praising my value as a woman
a brown woman
people claim is mad—
those doctors with their stethoscopes,
those nurses with their tablets
jotting down notes
to confine me in a cage
because I will not share
with them what I know.

I cannot tell you lies, cannot tell you I do not
hear voices rising from the silence in the desert,
angelic and beautiful voices
singing passionately from the onion
and the spirits
that I hear
telling me *Go on Rita, go on Rita,*
*even if no one knows we are here, if no one listens to us,*
*if no one believes we are,*
    *you have been blessed, you have been chosen*
*and so you walk, you walk to the blessed*
*love of our heart's music for your people.*

Hot chili, hot sun, hot sand, hot rocks,
that's where I go, into the hot searing lands
where life and creation is hot and blistering
I walk into that, happy and joyous
when I can endure the walk until I meet the
    hotness
of life, the whiteness of heat so hot and painful
that I hear in my soul the cries of my people
that ever hurt, that ever endured sorrow, that
    ever
experienced soul-tearing tragedy and in that
    moment and in that
day of delivery of our redemption
I have seen, no—
I am called upon to witness the worst of
    suffering,
and celebrate it with my walk, with my onion, my
    water, and my way of
        paying honor,
my way of dignifying their hurt, their pain, their
    destruction
is to walk on, keep walking, and walking.

Those are the spirits talking to me,
those are their ancestors speaking to me,
their suffering, their silence is their way of
    telling me
I should go north, keep walking, keep my
    silence,
let others call me mad, let others accuse me of
    leaving my children,
let others think the worst of me, but I must listen

174

to the voices that come from the sand, from the
    silence, from the emptiness
as it travels like an eagle through my soul,
    soaring
with screeching predatory cries
after me I willingly give myself
to it, open my arms and say here I am,
and then it leaves, it is afraid, it knows
I am sent by the spirits,
because of simple things I believe in—
chili, rice, prayer, hunger, love,
respect, truth,
and that is why I walk, that is why I don't talk.

*

I am Rita the mad woman,
the woman who betrayed her customs, who
    disappointed,
who people had trust to become a family
    woman,
Rita the Mestiza woman who dreams of her goats
    and sheep,
and the night she accidentally killed her husband,
who works hard,
who raised six children and who knows
three more children I have
from the divine world, given me by the gods
who tell me
that our culture is going to outlast all the lies
    and betrayals
all the money of men that come here and force
    us to grow

marijuana and poppy plants, force us at gun
   point to wake up
each morning and do the work we do not want
   to do.


I am Rita who sings
don't you know that my walking is a prayer for
   all of us
don't you know that my walking is a celebration
of our spirit,
that my walking is the string that connects us to
   the gods that care for us
that my walking is a great song without words
without sound without tears or laughter or
   smiles
or handshakes,
that my walk is our greatest fight against the
   traitors
that try to kill our souls, don't you know,
don't you know, is what my silence says,
is what my madness wants to convey to you smart
   people
who think you know everything, and have all the
   answers.
I am speaking to you through the gods' voices,
   their messages
come to you through me,
through this old gray haired tired woman,
   wrinkled face woman
that is worthless and has no value, no place in
   life,
don't you hear me, hear me, hear me.

\*

I am crazy because
I do not hate, because I do not hunger
for possessions, because I walk alone with my
    many souls
in a world made of people hating and warring
for more land.

    I am a woman with no borders, no gold
    only heart blood waves of energy,
    as I move across invisible boundaries into
        great understanding
    of life and people.

But they have accused me of being crazy
but here is what happened.

It is my soul that walks north,
to our ancestors' homeland, to where the blue
    cranes
carve air with feather chisels, as they go north
to my homeland,
my dreams of a homeland leap from my head
    and heart
like green skinned frogs, gorging themselves on
    insects of my desires
that buzz about my head all day and sting my
    flesh.

    The doctors did not understand this,
    how my toes are maize kernels
        my legs the stout stalks of corn

the pads of feet cracked and
   dried
  like arroyos in copper canyon
     that have had no water in years.
The nurse who smirked at me in the hospital
does not understand how many souls I have—

    she wanted to know about presidents and
     days
    and rational answers and facts to her
     questions
    but when I mentioned to her
    the time of the Aztecas, the Mayan love of
     corn,
    the Incan songs,
she scribbled in her notepad I was delusional
and I sulked, pretending to be mad
rather than have these soulless skins
    waste my time.
    Nor were they the only ones who shamed me.

*

My tribespeople
shamed me for leaving my village alone, for
  being alone in my misery,
for humiliating myself
by leaving without a man and in rags, with only
  an onion and water
jug for nourishment, heading north because I
  hear the voices and callings
of the Old Ones.

*178*

Nor were they the only ones who shamed
     me.
Dreams in green skins accompany me
leaping back and forth into reality and dream
with each footstep I take north, going across the
     desert,
the doctors asked me how I crossed
I told them the frogs helped me, leaping back
     and forth,
          frogs basking under nopalitos,
          burrowing in the cool sand
          moistened by deer urine,
          intoxicated by sage and creosote
          I walked from dawn 'til dusk
          thinking how frog's heart is a green
pumpkin seed
in my flesh
and with each step my heart
becomes a heavy yellow pumpkin.

At the end of the first moon cycle of walking
I felt lighter, I keep losing my tiny souls
in the desert, while my three big souls
get larger and larger until they tower over me
like hot air balloons, making footsteps light,
I walk north, hardly touching the ground,
lifted by my three souls, a stick-puppet dangling
     under them
held by spirit-string.     Wind
blows me back and forth, a ragged puppet kite
made of human hair and flesh,
that expands and wrinkles
as my large souls shrink.

*

How hunger became me.
Hunger in my sleep, in my dreams, in my
    imagined death,
in my spirit-illness,
hunger distributed through my body as if
    hunger were a stone
pushing out from every pore of my flesh,
root hairs under a turned over rock.

I go north to see the gringo land that was once
    ours,
I go north to study the gringos
I go north to hear them speak
I go north to tear myself from my Mestiza roots.
Reprimanded and scolded and shamed by my
    brothers and sisters
my own children turning their backs on me
the lawyers keeping all the money
from the court cases they filed on my behalf,
only the horny toads in desert brush welcome me,
only the coyote wags his tail at seeing me
only the wind combs my hair
only the sun caresses my flesh
only hunger makes love to my loins
open me up to make my footsteps in sand
a language of ritual
and this journey north is a ceremony to make
    me more woman,
more human, more mother, more earth, more
    universe,
more grass blade and hawk flight.

I am alive
because hunger breaks me in tortilla pieces
I am sober because hunger drinks my blood
still warm from the sword wound,
I am content because hunger bathes me in its
     morning dew
adding to my flowered soul the moisture for it to
     rise,
I am healthy because hunger
licks the succulent meat from my bones.

I feel the souls of the ancient come at me
from four directions
and each sits at my heart like hungry travelers
and I heap my heart high
with offerings of my visions, my dreams, my
     faith.
In return they permit me to visit my Aztec
     ancestors,
where I remember the many I am—

          How do I bring
          all aspects of Mestiza life
          over a thousand years
          into an old woman's heart
          and speak the meaning of it to others?

They laugh when I stare at them,
as hens in the butcher's grip
they begin each day
and as the sun falls each day
the butcher's blade falls.

I am made of moths and stars.

I walk north to recover my souls,
to recover my daughters, my sons, my parents,
    my sisters,
millions of them who have vanished into air,
into moths and stars, I come to recover them,
bring back their dreams to the Mestiza people
so we are not separate from earth.

I want the moths and stars to walk home with
    me.
I want us to walk together to church, to my
    brother's house,
to my sister's maize beer making party
to share our stories and reclaim our voices again.

I want to dance, to laugh, to fish, to recite
    poetry.
I am Rita, the one who strays, one who dropped
    from the sky
to challenge the sorcerers who would steal and
    harm our souls.

I go beyond me in my walk,
it empowers me,
when I walk I see my dreams
become lizards
blinking in the shade of cacti and stone,
when I walk I am the black butterfly
deeply indulging fully in flight
and the delight of floating on air
knowing it will die tomorrow.

My wings have developed so I can fly
fully immersed in pure joy for a day
then tomorrow die, a lyric in a song
carried off by the wind.

    I have words in me thirsty to speak
    for centuries now,
    feelings in me thirsty to express themselves
    for centuries now,
    dreams in me thirsty to make real
    for centuries now.

And that is why I walk north,
to know more of myself as I become more of
   myself
I become more.

\*

"I never knew this thirst could so completely
overtake me to a point where I would have given
   my life
for a drop of water. I never knew that about
   water . . ."

    that is what I told the psychiatrist and
      doctors
    at the hospital in Kansas.

They found me rummaging through a
   refrigerator
in a house. I was a stranger they said, in a house
picking through food in a refrigerator.

*183*

Others had sighted me along the road,
sleeping, walking, standing
and they all wondered who I was, how I had
   crossed the desert,
and how I had made it across the border.

The answers flow with water,
rush, brimming every field,
carrying debris, splitting seeds to blossom
   abundant crops,
carousing in channels and tumbling down
   tributaries
broadening out into pools and shallows
then gaining momentum and energy
raging, raging, raging
in my veins, my mouth, my heart.

If I encounter you on the road,
as mother I bless you
with a crucifix around your neck,
feed you agave hearts, water in a gourd dipper,
     and move on,
      called by the prophecies in ancient books
      their voices in my head, shoulders, elbows,
       wrists and palms.

As a woman who heals
I offer you cuts of goat meat
roasted underground for three days and nights,
an earthen jar of maize beer,
a willow sapling, a patio and wooden plank
   bench
to rest yourself on.

As human, I offer you my heart
which is semicircle,
opening to all who need comfort and love.

I come from canyon lands in Chihuahua,
kindling memories aflame,
illuminate myself as a girl when I roamed
freely through the canyons singing old songs,
my running feet rasping sticks on a gourd
keeping time to soul song,
I offer boiled chickens, blankets, ground maize,
to the Gods for blessings.

\*


    They asked me why I left my village,
      what possessed me to journey to Kansas,
and of course of my feet during those years I
   walked
how the bones had reshaped themselves to
   contours
of desert paths, how my toes curved to grip dirt
on coyote and deer trails,
     and during the doctors' questions, the
       lawyers'
     sly-eyed cynical interrogation
     implying I was some sort of terrorist
       or madwoman,
all I could remember was the terrible thirst I
   endured.
I never knew thirst could so wholly consume
   your souls and body,

so completely absorb every thought and sight
   and sound and smell,
      scratching my throat like a dried corncob
      in my mouth like a shriveled mushroom
      clawing into my lips like scorpions
      digging into my heels like steel-toothed bear
         traps,
      burrowing into my belly button
      like a diamond drill head,
      snaking through the bone marrow of my
         skeleton
      until I succumbed to it completely and
         became thirst:

My name was thirst,
my white onion and empty water jug were
   thirst,
my Chihuahua desert was thirst,
my God was called thirst,
      picturing my children I imagined them as
         raindrops,
      seeing mirages beyond in the wavering
         heat of midday
      I rushed to bathe in waterfalls,
      a vulture in the sky was a glass of water
            settling on a rock
            shimmering coldly,
         my tongue turned to a wooden
            spatula,
         the wood cracked, splintered
            swelled,
            was hard as a brick I scratched at

with my fingernails
and I laughed,
a thirsty laugh
drowning in so much thirst.

*

Sometimes so thirsty and hungry
I became sick, vomited and had diarrhea.
    I scratched up roots and scrubbed my scalp
    with stone and sand.
Dehydration left me weak and stunned by sun,
I walked in circles in a glowing orb of light,
chanting my grandfather's owl drum songs.
I saw my ancestors arrive. I was in a field of light,
dogs and goats and cattle in the golden fields,
my auntie Juanita and uncle Torrez,
    they made tortillas, came in from the fields
    with arms full of corn, sweet, healthy, yellow
        corncobs.
Then I woke from my delirium,
my face caked with dirt, ants and bugs in my
    hair,
cactus needles in my fingers and arms,
    blood all over me.


The next day I reentered the place where thirst
    and hunger rule,
danced beneath hail and lightning,
sage fields hit by lightning, burning
    all around sage smoldering
    myself in the center of burning sage fields
    as if I was an offering to God.

Old gray haired wrinkled Mestiza woman
gone mad, straying away from her village,
abandoning her family
to wander in the desert
is what they reported in the newspapers.
The devil has his workers—
A writer wrote a play about me,
imagining what my jailers and counselors
    said,
how the nurse was, the attitudes of
    authorities and judges
especially lawyers, brutes
without compassion or imagination.

Should I have told them the truth?
That I was called on by my ancestors
to perform this ritual, to cleanse the souls
of those who chose to forget the earth-laws
those who forgot the balance of life,
    I walk in 120 degree heat
    not alone,
    but speaking with plant tribes,
    that have cured me in the past with fever,
    head colds, measles,
        some appear on air as beautiful women,
        handsome men,
    most appear as mist beings.

I am from the people of Rejogochi,
    my own people thought I was bewitched
    but I am not afraid of anyone
    and have no need to avenge anyone
        for only I have harmed myself

by believing in the voices,
in the prophecies,
in the words of our ancestors
and the beauty of our songs and dances.
People knew my mother
carried me sideways in her womb
and she kept a clay bowl of parched maize
next to the door,
she scattered hot chili powders in the house
to keep sorcerers away,
she marked my forehead with sage ash
to keep the devil from taking my souls,
because I was different,
I heard the ancient voices
and followed the ancient trail back to our
origins,
to Aztlan's Seven Caves, Blue Heron land,
and took my thousand mile walk to cure my
culture.

My father bathed my body in cedar and juniper
smoke,
and the Mexican government and Jesuits
denounced me
as a mad hag, a babbling fool
when I uttered ancient prayers,
when I grew mushrooms in my stomach, when I
spit out
a small stone and worms,
and when I flew in my peyote visions.
        I saw my people singing on a mountaintop,
and they instructed me to walk, walk north,
plant your feet in Aztlan

bury your heart in Blue Heron fields,
give your souls to the seven caves like burial
  bones
ground to meal and mixed with water and eaten.
        The doctor's analysis
        was that I was mad.
        They forced me to take sedatives
        pills that made me sleep for months.
My medicine people
thought my souls had been kidnaped
but truly it's the souls of other that have been
  corrupted
           and kidnaped.


Had I words to say what I feel,
the poet in me would tell you
how I passed through cities
cafes and restaurants filled with people
gorging, while two blocks either way
children slept in cardboard boxes and mothers
  sold their infants;
kings of the land were the drug dealer
driving luxury SUVs, Cadillacs, and BMWs,
sports stars bedding down with fourteen-year-old
  girls
movie stars trading money and diamonds for
  virgins and drugs,
bankers laundering money for corporate
  gangsters,
     no one cares; no one remembers their
      mother memories,

no one turns to their neighbors in
    compassion,
it's all blood and greed and lies and betrayals
    and destruction,
        city after city I passed
        I saw this, heard and felt it, smelled
        gutters with young girls
        worming their way around for crack,
        saw the black and brown and white
            thugs
        raping and killing and numbing their
            brains
        with shocks of crack,
        I paused in front of storefront windows
        banked with TVs
        and saw the killing in Afghanistan and
            Iraq,
        saw the Twin Tower corpses shoveled up,
        saw Enron and Anderson accounting
            firm and others
        rob, steal, lie, cheat and destroy
            millions of people's retirement
                savings,
        and you accuse me of being crazy?

I, Rita, who fell from the sky,
entered my ancient lands of Atzlan, to re-create
    myself
in the sacredness of each footstep
hard toes brittle and scaly like a female wolf,
I come as warrior woman you despise, ridicule,
    scorn,

my bones ancient flutes humming my song of
    peace, forgiveness and love.
Don't you know! Can't you see! Listen, hear the
    Gods!
With my onion bag and plastic milk jug of water
I walk past your TVs, your mansions, your
    gluttonous ways,
your snarling over drugs and money and
    possessions.
In the midst of this I re-create myself—
    walk like sperm toward the egg-sun
    and my development begins, anew, male/
        female,
    mad and crazed in the belly of sinful life,
    fertilized by women from ancient ways
    carried in the current of wind and dust,
    carrying me gently toward the womb
    as I divide into many women,
    woman at the street corner woman carrying
        a briefcase
    woman pushing her baby carriage, woman
        jogging,
    more and more divisions of me take place
    until I am everyone
    until I am in the birth canal of creation
    re-creating myself into all of you.

I burrow into life,
into the sunlight, into the moonlight, into the cacti,
attach myself to the cells of the horny toad's
    tongue

and suck vital nourishment from the stones,
   sand, leaves, cacti spines,
that forms in me a new brain, a new spine, new
   nerves and skin,
wind forms my heart again,
water shapes my blood,
sky my muscles and the earth my skeleton.
   This is who I am, Rita, from the sky,
rumbling with ancient ancestors' voices,
      and eventually, under the stars
      as I rest on dirt,
      I am reshaped,
my heart twitches anew, beats again with
   renewed vigor.

*


I keep walking north, to my ancient lands,
push forward, hungry, thirsty, seeking life, push
up, my arms bud out, I rapidly gain size,
grow new in this world north of my village,
as people laugh at me, mistrust me,
accuse me, suspect me.

I cry in the dark, I am without parents,
am utterly alone,
but I go on, my lungs expand,
my face now made, grooved out by God's clay-
   shaping fingers,
my ears grown out, I am amazed at my fingers
   again,
and know

that is why I came north,
to remake myself, to follow the ancient works of
    God,
allow myself to be made anew
into one we are all, filled with tears and laughter,
but they spit at me,
diagnose me as stupid and insane,
while my tongue creates a new language, my
    tongue
stretching and pulling words
to make things all around physical,
I have knees now; I slowly stand up against these
    mockers,
dig my heel and toes into the ground against
    these scoffers,
my eyelids blink in the cold harsh wind,
as I move onward, following the internal map of
    my heart
toward home, until I am joined together with
    home,
joined to the plants and birds and air and fire,
until I am one with creation.

And in Kansas,
I surrendered myself as your prisoner,
        Rita, fallen from the sky . . .


*


I didn't go north with weapons
no sticks, rocks, knives or guns
filled my pockets,
no deception, lies or betrayals

bulged my heart,
no reason to fight or imprison others.
                    Instead,
on an afternoon when clouds poured
earth gouging gully washers
in arroyos,
I threw myself in the stream
and the raging water transformed
itself into a young black bear that kept me afloat,
                    cottonwood saplings
transformed into coyotes dragged me up
by my arms and legs onto the bank,
and there, coughing up gulps of water
            I thanked the young black bear,
            I bowed to cottonwoods,
re-born from their hands into a freer life,
I walked again, all day and night, humming
prayers to Peyote People,
that they care for my many newer souls.

In towns and cities I passed
I smoked myself with sage and mesquite,
warding off city ways, its corrupt intents—
            keep your incest, your greed,
            your mistrust, your cynicism.
I do not come north to prey on your possessions,
piled so high now
they obscure and block the gates of salvation.

There is nothing but an open path to my gates,
            clear passage,
            where I consecrate my life to my
            creators

offering each of the cardinal directions
each evening a spoonful
of ground maize,
four pieces of tortilla, four maize
kernels, and four
uncooked pinto beans.
At dawn, holding my rosary and crucifix in my
hand
I pray and continue my thousand mile walk
north.
I would have loved to have met Mother
Teresa
who did the same.
I moved through the outskirts of cities
where ugly sights of gangs and poverty
racism and privilege
cut off fresh roses from my heart's garden
and I hang the shriveled bouquets
on doorknobs
as my symbol of lost innocence.
Each city is
an underworld of lewd caprice, a playground
to waste life in orgies and drugs, sex and money.

You drive past me, rummaging through
trashcans
see a diseased old woman,
bent over stooped corpse on the highway
shoulder,
you think
I might be good washing your clothes, perhaps
cleaning your house,

low pay and low maintenance, but my clothing
is too dirty, my speech unintelligible,
I frighten you,
I smell of juniper and cedar smoke,
    and it's true, perhaps
    I am dead,
    perhaps this is my death walk,
filled as my starving mind is
with goat, mutton and chicken, beans, quelites,
maize tortillas,
  maybe I am dead
  and this walk is my death walk
  maybe, when you talk to me, question me,
   interrogate me,
  all of you are communicating with dead
for it seems to me as I look out from my weary eyes
your lives are death rituals,
death ceremonies,
death celebrations,
death lovers,
  offering your gold and power and killing
   machines
  to death,
  murdering Palestinian babies, Afghanistan
   mothers,
  imprisoning young Iraq men and women for
   life,
  distributing crack to kill young beautiful
   minds
maybe,
as I stand here behind the Hilton hotel

searching in the dumpster
    I peer at you on the outside bar patio
    by the pool,
    maybe you are all dead,
is that insane of me to think this
considering the evidence?
    Am I mad
    when I see cemeteries filled with more
      young
    than old people,
am I mad
when I see those who don't work have the
  money
and those who work all day
die of starvation?
    Am I mad when I see the rich lawyers
    and politicians lie and cheat and swindle
      and extort
    and never get punished
    while a starving boy steals an apple
    gets twenty years in prison?
    Am I mad
    that doctors won't treat children because
     they have no
    insurance

    does this knowledge certify me as mad
        if I see this with my own eyes
            and label it and share this bad
            news with others?

Insane?
I would, if it helped bring back sanity,
douse myself with gas on the courthouse lawn
and set myself on fire—
but they don't care if an old woman burns,
don't care about so much anymore, they thrive
            on bloody spectacle
      on gory gruesome crime scenes,
      on cruel and barbaric entertainment—
so, instead,
I walk, and walk and walk,
making my walk a prayer for all humanity,
for our salvation, our redemption,
because the Lord has suffered so much for me,
      I too wish to give away what I have
and along the way
to honor the Lord's suffering for me,


I gave my few clothes to the church,
took the wool and cloth and blankets I had
and gave them to my neighbors,
what few coins, three stones and bead necklaces
   I had,
the hoe, one plow disc,
a chisel, a mule yoke, a dull ax,
      ears of white maize in a sack,
      two wooden balls and sticks and hoops
            for the footraces,
            three used candles,
            and gave them all away
            before heading out to the desert alone
            to make my thousand mile trip
            on foot.

It felt so good to do that,
and while others called it mad,
    labeled me insane for doing so,
    it felt so good
    I became so light, I floated up,
        I became Rita Falling from the Sky.

# Smoking Mirrors

A.

I come out of the south,
from the darkness
    where death ferments in the dawn,
seeping from limbs, moistening
what is hard and cold and alone at night.
Out of the darkness
    like a dream,
    a storm beneath my flesh
        two faces,
        two bodies,
        a hybrid flower
            of honey and poison,
            half moon half sun,
            intoxicated on fragrance
                stinking of sweat
                smooth and rough
                bearded and hairless
                with penis and vagina
                two mouths
            constantly quarreling
                two tongues

twenty fingers
and twenty toes
in constant conflict
two of us,
blurred at birth by some cruel god,
always alone,
out of the dark like an extinct
animal
my body a cave
I look out from
at night,
see my red eyes.
My sharp teeth, my red heart
bleeding,
I can easily kill as surrender to you,
kiss or bite,
smile or snarl,
because I am made of two
opposite and similar to myself
a field of yellow flowers
and cactus.

B.

In a strange way, I give and take life—
yes, what you would call this whore,
this freak of nature,
this hideous beast
gives and takes life.
You're so fickle, so easily manipulated; you are
mere feather I saw
in my hands on hot days.
I am a snake, sloughing skins

friend of the dark,
slithering in low life streets
arching with fangs that fill you with sweet venom
as you gasp for breath
as you aching vow all your love for me
     until you discover
      I am you, and something in you dies, you turn
      into a destroyer, maiming and murdering
        my kind.
And I withdraw beneath your beatings
beneath your raging fist,
       your macho revenge spills onto me
       with your secrets and loves and
        whispered sins
       I cradle in my bleeding mouth
       I cherish in the embrace of my broken
        ribs.

C.

I destroy your ideas
your view of the world,
of the way things should be.
At night, in my world
blue becomes black
red becomes yellow
man is woman
light and dark blurs,
moon is the sun, night is the day
when I come out.

I let go of the rope
and you fall, fall into

the entrails of my life
and with gentle, caressing hands
I crush your view of the world.

D.


You do not understand
how much pain I am in—
memories of myself as a boy
confused by being born different
than other boys,
shame gutted me, created in me
a dark hole that each day I died in,
while other children's lives were played in the
    parks,
I crouched behind a headstone
        in the cemetery and wept my shame out—
        while other boys watched TV on couches
        I was drawn to dance on broken alley crates
        where lecherous men and women seduced
            me.
I survived my two sexed divine disease,
deceiving friends and drug fiends,
lying in bed with an innocent lover
my sheets become my vile plumage
where I gorge on his love with vulture'd hunger,
ecstatic pilgrim whose shrine is the male body
male sighing after coming, male gripping my ass
male pounding from behind
male kisses, rough and horrible
filled with pain,
        o the pain/pleasure
        of men's passion

as they pillage my heart
open me
adore me
honor me
and devour me
in their hatred and their love.

And then the dream is over,
and seeing my face stubble,
studying with contempt my manly features
in the mirror,
as if from my grave, I wake to the dawn

yearning for the night again
when I'll sing sweetly to charm
    men's lewd attention,
    lure the cobra from the basket
    to my music.

Not the reflection in the mirror
will they see
nor me plucking my eyes out,
nor the wrinkles on my male face,
but opening my compact mascara case,
pulling out my eye liners, tweezers,
the mirror will begin to open
like a dark curtain
for the actress to appear
I transform into a young sensuous girl,
my lemony breasts evoke their dizzying delight,
yes,
    obsessed with my flesh, my lust, my body

the curved wings of my thighs, my hips and
   legs,
float across their hearts like quetzal birds
filled with voodoo omens
of sexual fulfillment.

Thrones and furs are what I desire,
down filled beds and comforters,
popular, sought after, that even flamenco guitars
wail their lust and passion for me,
walking under peach tress,
      through flower gardens,
      I forget the back seat cars
      as a sweaty whore,
         turning tricks for American servicemen's
            twenty dollar bills.

I open my legs to the moon,
      rings on each of my fingers,
      call me your witch,
         as I kiss you
         strip my clothes off,
make this night for me, for you,
         as if we were both falling
         falling into a world
         filled with happiness,
         and not us, as we are,
            looking for love,
   for a man
      to love me,
         to love me,
            to love me . . .

E.

Living in squalid quarters,
cracked stucco walls, decrepit ceiling peeling
    paint—
lurid colors of purple, blue, black,
        gives their rooms an eerie menacing aspect
where our darkest secrets are unveiled, indulged
    in,
            and then,
the change—
        the long black hair is brushed out
        they strip off grimy t-shirts
            to reveal supple but firm breasts,
            lipstick is applied to their curved lips,
and the blossoming begins,
            rare flowers un-petal
            their skin is shaved smooth and softer
                    than Asian silk
            the area around their eyes blushed blue,
                outlined black
            they become cats,
            and sitting nude in a chair as they
                stretch their black stockings
            up their legs,
                urges assault the viewers' loins
                fantasies unravel like spools of red
                    yarn
                caught in claws of flame,
and quickly the mouth
that was some construction worker's mouth
becomes Marilyn Monroe's puckering tease,

the face takes on seductive shadows
that draw the light to their cheeks and
   nose
in a way a traveler glimpses distant bays
   of glistening waters
            pools of emerald waters
            multicolored reefs
               shimmer below;
they stare back at you,
the way a black jaguar might stare at you,
the moon throwing shadows of leaves and vines
on its face,
its lips blood red, open lazily, almost inhaling
   your soul,
its eyes black orbs of caves you enter
      to discover the bones of ancestors,
         the eyelids narrowed, luring you in to
            their
               world of sex, laughter, death,
                  temporal renewal
                     from your desperate life,
                     squeezing as they slowly blink
                     bitter remorse and betrayals
                     from your heart;
but the light that falls on their cheeks,
   gives them a rising dawn of innocence
      where all your life's accusers
      evaporate into mist,
      they become vulnerable
      and draw you out from your blues
      like Eric Clapton's guitar
      at dawn, wailing and ripping chords
      in a New Orleans dew-dripping street

where you want to take this girl's hand
and beat down doors that have signs Closed
hanging on them,
singing the morning
so everybody wakes up to your nectarine
perversions,
and it doesn't matter, finally
that you get drunk or high
or that you've spent the rent money
and lied to your woman at home,
because the magic these transvestites sprinkle
over you
blinds you for night,
you don't have to think about having
nothing to look
forward to,
not your menial labor,
not your boring life,
nor that you're just another face in the
streets
another silver toothed mouth,
and set of lips grimly pursed
enduring pain,
caught in an O of
horror,
about to speak but fearful,
about to cry out but you can't,
because once these women
flutter their complacent, honeyed smile at
you,
your private thoughts like flies get caught
in the sweetness
and behind your eyes,

everything you've learned from hard experience,
is left behind,
     and close your eyes
     and go baby, go with the current
     of the river
     never knowing where it originates or ends,
     trusting her,
          you shatter the bridges
          of your life
          and head out for open sea
          into the hurricane of your lust.


F.


It's sad to be this way
to know you're a woman
     yet awkwardly stride about town
          in a man's body,
it's sad
to want to dance and your male body
gets in the way, spills over
with crude movements like a bucket of water
     spilling over
yes, it's sad,
you feel damned, cursed,
and there's no escaping holding this man's hand
  I am
like his mother and escorting him
to the market,
     trailing behind me everywhere,
     he watches me, he suspects me of
          abandoning him,
     sometimes he's cruel, and when I weep

he stands back and laughs at me,
yet I know,
I am nothing without him,
my benevolent tormentor,
the enemy that knows my every move,
and what plans I have to escape him
he knows even before I can think them.
I guess in my tears
we meet as friends
we embrace each other sadly,
he becomes kin, no more finger pointing,
and I attend to him,
our emotions like a secret entryway
which we use to retreat from the pain,
the tears, the hurt,
of being together all the time.

No one understands how we feel,
yet, he understands
how I imagine my denim workman's shirt
to be an Inca gown of a princess
and when he wakes up brutish and growling,
I understand his pain
how he would like to be rid of me,
go south to his village in Mexico and retrieve his
life,
meet his old friends,
go out into the fields and join them in work.
But it's not to be,
we are tied together as sure as were convicts
chained and hobbled
forever. There is no escaping our prison cell.
There is no date when the sentence will expire.

He's tattooed the Sacred Heart of Christ on
   his back
which I have tolerated,
imagine,
      in bed when I'm loving a man,
      and the man asks about the tattoo,
how can I explain
it is not my skin, not my tattoo,
      that my flesh is made of air, of mirrors,
      of stones and dirt,
         how do I explain to my lover
         that my bed is a small canoe
            and my kisses are flowers
            I toss on the water
            in his honor.

You see,
my prayers have never been answered,
I have never been restored to my original self,
I don't know who I am or how I got here—
somewhere, the angel,
      that was supposed to look over me,
      got drunk and fell off a cliff,
      and there is not one to help me,
      so I offer a red-lipped smile at the world
         and a few people know
         the smile is a wound.

G.

There is this stark sadness,
the stench about this life,
      that lingering trace that I am mad,

that it's all a bad, sorrowful nightmare.
I have blue linoleum floors,
a blue bed I sit on to clasp my black anklets,
and who knows
    how long can I carry on—
    what will happen when I get old,
    when my beauty fades like an old pair of
        shoes
    with heels shaved down,
    me wobbling bow-legged down the sidewalk
    with little boy throwing stones at me?
A cheap fan cools my heated bones.
Smoking a pipe now and then relieves the
    presence of the stranger that
always seems to be there,
            staring at me in the mirror.
Not God, not saints, not folk cures,
nothing can help me anymore—

these pink walls, these clown faces, these colors
I paint myself with are the witnesses to my life,
and no one will notice when I'm gone,
stabbed in the heart one night
in bed by a jealous lover
    but until that time,
    I dance on the small stage,
    and I believe I am someone else,
    believe that none of that will come to pass.
There's never been anyone to talk to,
so I talk to the clown faces,
we pretend we are on some stage, in some
    theater in New York

or Los Angeles,
    that we do not live on our knees,
    that we do not fear the day,
    that we are on stage singing to a full house,
    and a wealthy man falls in love with us,
    and takes us away to live in a big house,
        yes the dream,
I suckle like a babe at its tit,
gorging myself on its milk,
fattening myself each night
because the days are so bleak and lean
that sometimes
    I feel dead,
    I feel my life carried in a coarse wooden
      casket
    through the streets
        a monster that finally died,
        a monster that lived behind doors,
        that given us by life,
        and that made us worse than we ever
          thought we
        could be.
So just to be,
    is enough, with our bountiful baskets of gifts
      we once had to offer to life,
    which we emptied at the disgraceful landfill,
    which we gave away for small dusty awards,
    with the grief of lepers everywhere
        we go,
    chased away so we must live in darkness,
    here in this trashed out place I call home,
      we'll believe is my beautiful palace
        and you I,

for a moment, will believe,
what we do, is love
and not drown, in our sadness,
not drown in our sadness.

Let us be honorable as
those stray dogs roaming fence-lines
snatching white pigeons midair,
slouching under a tree to feast on their
catch,
let's scatter our feathers my angels
everywhere,
growling at intruders as we crush the
bones
of each other's hearts;
and have our romance played out in the
cemetery
visiting those like us we'll call our relatives,
quietly sitting over the graves weeping,
as traffic hums on the freeway in the
distance,
let's pretend our voices are children's again
and pretend we believe in a Christmas,
taping paper reindeer and snowflakes to
windows,
believing outside Santa was watching me.
and Baby Jesus really is being born,
nestled in mangers of our straw hearts,
you and I are the shepherds
came out only at night
loved in the dark so no one could see
my face,
screamed and cried in a voice no one

heard,
lost herself
in hair-blowers, curtains, music, black
    leather outfits,
empty rooms,
like an angel with wings butchered,
mangy hair,
tossed out of heaven,
    to exist in rock-rubbled crumbling
        graffiti walls
    even stray dogs avoid,
    or industrial raftered buildings
    intended to store fifty gallons of toxic
        waste,
    or converting factory workers'
        bathrooms,
    with stained sinks, I,
    somehow, pretend it's my extravagant
        dressing room,
    and the torn mattresses and busted
        windows
            and ripped screens,
blood stained floors, warped water-logged
    cardboard walls,
become my palace,
where my heart grows like a spiny yucca
    cactus,
and paper roses sprout
in blood that blooms from heart wounds.

Here, you see, Gods are blind
here where I live I've sewn God's lips shut
with threads of my black pubic hair,

here I've cut God's hands off that never reached
  out to bless me,
here I've taken a hammer and crushed the
  religious idols,
here, when you come to see me, drunken,
    seeking sex or company,
    you'll find no Gods reproaching us
    for what we do,
    because when you come here to visit me,
    it's the page in the book
    that was torn out—
        so under the black blankets of my bed,
        we invent the story we desire,
        we imagine the story
        with a kinder ending.

## Singing at the Gates

No Pope nor Priest could more enhance my life
than Mechica smiles and Inca eyes,
those startled sparrow eyes peering over papa's
   nesting-shoulder,
entering the Santuario, her father's back to me,
      the brown baby girl hugging his neck,
      her face pressed against his white shirt
        collar,
as it has been for a thousand years,
from Mayans, Incans, Aztecas, Mexicans,
   Chicanos,
      Cholos y Homies,
we've carried and carry our infants through
   government massacres, forced marches
          off our lands,

to the present in fiestas, low-rider gatherings,
   our children
      clinging to our arms and bodies for safety,
        a continuous unseen line from the
          beginning of our Mestizo birth,
        walking across America,
        long before white men arrived,

our arms circle our loved ones,
imperfect and beautiful,
in NY baseball shirt, chain and crucifix down
our chest, La Ruca
wearing Brown Pride workout t-top,
black net-gloves wrist to elbow,
tandito hat with feather,
tight black shorts, bobby socks,
platform spike heels,
low-riding
mamacita down for
the dream cruise.

Y pues, look around and see the pensive
sombrero'd rancheros con palos en los
fieles,

scooping shovel after shovel of
dirt
cleaning la acequia—
soil-scent fills your nostrils aging veterano,
and I wonder what palabras are whispered
to you by the rain
y el viento,
sage, yierba, alfalfa, calabacitas,
boots and jeans worn down and faded by
day-long plowing.

In cities along the Rio Grande,
Burque, Santa, Espa, Taos, y Cruces,
locos scrawl graffiti duels, branching on
adobe walls predicting

a cold and deadly winter,
    y mujeres gather at la cantina for a
    wedding, clap and sing,
    close eyes, open mouths, faces 'pa la
    musica,
    so much erotic sensuality in their waists
    and legs y nalgas!

    Backpack Chicano students roam plaza
    crowds
    where senoritas flick Spanish fans over
    heavy lidded eyelashes,
    las ninas tie roses in their hair,
    madrecitas clutch home-spun woolen
    shawls,
    crowds tip-toe to see the singer and
    musicians,
    while the woman in the wedding dress
    leans
        toward the photographer,
        rosary weaving through her fingers,
        silver crown on her turreted hair,
        white of her teeth whiter
        than her wedding dress.

    I sing at the gates about the beauty of
    my people,
  while police arrest a boy for wearing his
  baseball cap
    cocked to the side,
stigmatized thug for wearing a goatee and
  mustache,
      tattoo of the archangel Gabriel

on his arm,
chain around his neck,
NIKE hoop shirt,
leaning against a '45 coupe door, hood muraled
with Tonantzin,
sunglassed jainas with long black hair
chilling inside,
I praise them for never having forgotten
their cultura
or ancestral roots, wearing papa's hand-me-
down khakis,
warmed by a woodstove, surrounded with
pious paintings
y mama's weaving loom,
some eventually lose their land to casino
slots,
some mourned at roadside altars senselessly
murdered,
where I kiss the wreathes on barbwire
fences
and sign myself in prayer, march behind
three priests
bearing crucifixes in procession,
and after solemn benedictions,
sit my woman on my knee and fondle her
breasts in their memory.
I praise cowboys swinging their ropes,
soft leather saddle rubbing
with the horse's clip-clop,
take my youngest son to the Matachines
dances
in the sacred Chicano pueblo,

pass the Mayan turquoise jaguar
   mask
three thousand years old around
   and fast for days,
pray and sing pray and sing pray
   and sing,
for the five-year-old girls in Flamenco
   dancer's hoop skirts
ruffling hems high as they kick and give the
   rooster's yelp,
serape adults clap and hats fly,
while old men kneel before the rebel priest
   wearing a well-used cowboy hat,
flanked by two stout men
holding candle staffs aloft praising the
   cottonwood tree.

   I amble past barrio yards
where vandals hammered statues to
   smithereens,
         beheaded Jesus,
         trampled fencing as they fled,
         and I recall
I started my learning from tio Solis,
his small adobe home displaying more
   religious statues than a church,
the special one—El Nino de Atocha, had his
   own small alcove and altar,
mat for shoes, tiny pictures of our familia y
   la plebe on the walls,
carvings of La Malinche, Cortes' puta, who
   rather than let him

send her kids to Spain for an education,
              drowned them
              in Rio Grande.

        I learned dancing with gypsies, old men
              in suits, ribbons,
wooden swords and tin mirrors, and I danced
past crumbling adobes, rusting truck hulls y el
    campo santo,
              in knee-high weeds,
              wearing my feathered bishop's
                  bonnet,
              scrolled with paper, I scuffed
              my cheap black shoes in dust and
                  gravel singing
              he-he-ho-na-no
              all the way down to the twilight
                  river-trails,
following the young girl in white crinoline first-
    communion dress,
asking Spirits to bless her journey.

        No mountain hawk has more courage or
              fierce truth
than the Vatos that come from north and south
    and east and west
tattooed low-riders dressed in swaying cloths like
    Mayan healers,
who've walked beside mothers to a hundred
    burials
for young locos shot by police or rival gangs,
who kneel to take rocks from the dirt to make
    crosses

for fallen brothers and sisters, rock crosses all
   over Aztlan,
      symbolizing union, faith, identity.

   Generation after generation—
La Raza's people-priest wears a bandanna
stations himself among la gente, rattling our
   tambourines,
      wearing our Matachine mask,
      from ancient ninety-year-old abuelitas
who make who we are burn bright, unfold and
   rumble deep,
      deep rumble to the young altar boy
         peering through the crowd for his
            cousin,
               deep rumble to the Chicana nun
                  kissing Christ's feet,
                  deep rumble as we unfurl
                     banners of San Martin
and San Ysidro Labrador, who gives our fields
   abundant harvest,
      to the Penitentes in moradas chanting
         ancient Moorish/Indio alabados
      by candlelight, to La Palomia in a hundred
         small churches
            kneeling in pews
            appealing to Christ for mercy,
               murmuring
            the deep rumble of our love.

   We stand together great and small,
mentally ill next to the lesbian aunt,
pinto next to the school teacher,

twelve-year-old tecato's daughter next to the
  community center fighter,
mother with a hundred lovers next to ese
  who vows never to retreat, proud
Santero with his retablos, firme bato,
    I lose myself in all of you,
in the tiniest capilla in the furthest reach of
  el llano
for an infant who never survived the harsh
  winter
because there was no medicine,
    I am the sand beneath its head,
    the bonfire log that flames in a man's
      backyard
    as he stands with stick in hand, thinking
      of his life,
    the widow who proudly shows off her
      mother's photograph
    framed in wood she whittled and shaved
      herself.


    I celebrate you, the virtues and customs
      you have defended
    despite colonialists rampaging to kill
      every one of you—
    you survived, madre clinging to babes in
      arms
    and kneeling before crosses,
    you survived hefe hoisting your sons on
      your shoulders and riding
    them around the yard,
    you survived amante waiting outside
      church for your novia,

you survived ninos playing in church
yards, on steps, rails,
you survived vato loco
with hat and tank-top t-shirt,
polished shoes,
leaning on haunches,
an arm on crooked leg,
very cool, beside your
chromed out
low-rider,
you survived abuelita smiling under the apple
tree,
so grand and open and happy a smile it's
like a wheat field on fire,
singing our skill with mud and rock in
building adobes,
our carving the finest figures of wood,
our cultivating fields to offer huge
crops.

Intact is the older brother's love for the
younger,
intact is love proving we are men and dying
foolishly,
pistiando with our compas and fighting each
other,
sometimes killing one another,
our cultural past and heritage runs though
the boys
wrapped in thick coats and beanie caps riding
their horses,
in the cowboy strumming his electric guitar

and the young fat apple-cheeked boy in a
  hooded sweatshirt,
in the brother and sister picking pinons in the
  mountains,
    in the kids
        burning rubber on their bicycles in the
        church parking lot,
in the two elderly women dressed in black
        with iron strong hearts and
          hummingbird soulwings,
          old and new merge, expand and spread,
riding tractors and low-riders and Harleys, t-shirt
  and leathers,
lost in fiesta crowds or alone on a porch,
still using woodstoves and suspenders, still
  working at the railroad yards,
in greasy and smoke-charred overalls, capped
  and stubbled,
decaying hundred-year-old ranch houses crack
  and splinter on the prairie,
while grandchildren of farmers who lived there
march in urban streets chanting no war no war,
    and newborns scream their arrivals,
    and fathers with wrist chains and tattoos
    cling to their little loves at parks,
    and the circle widens and expands and
      ripples
      toward every closed gate, with tribal drums
      beating,
      gourds blowing and rattles rattling
      we are here, we are here, we are here,

hue hue te otl, hue hue te otl, hue hue te
    otl,
that we have always been here.

Unfolding my lips to sing your beauty and
    resilience
an agave giant petals
holding you all like desert raindrops,
moistening your thirst for freedom and
    respect,
quenching your hearts to bloom at every
    entrance
        gate and door
        in every city.

# JULIA

I am Julia,
   a little girl
   who breathes in air
   and feels butterflies in my stomach,
      who skips the dirt paths
      between friends' houses
      and hears songs in the earth
      whispering their love to me.

I kiss you—
   my lips are red blossoms
   trembling with dew.
      I don't know where I get this happiness
      to praise life, to praise my mother and
        father
      to deflect mean energy that would
        bruise my soul
      to celebrate the sparrow's chirping,
      to pray so hard sometimes
      because I see how people hurt
      and in the songs of my blood
      I am able to sing their words for them,
    share my songs with them,
      they stand at my door,

mouth agape in awe
of this gift to feel their heart's hurt.
When my cousins' father and mother
abandoned them
in their yard I hold my cousins' hands, grasp
them tight
whirl them in mine,
we turn we turn we turn
join with all creatures
living in life of the moment, to release our
suffering,
surrender ourselves to the breeze
is what I teach and spirits have taught
me.
And to fight—
not with fist, not with angry words, not with
mean attitude—
but the way yellow sunflowers fight their way up
to sunlight,
the way the trout flail their way upstream in the
Chama river,
the way the elm and cottonwood trees unclench
each mighty leaf at dawn
to defy the dark night,
welcoming dawn with a fluttering dog's wage
welcoming sunrise with barks,
welcoming sounds and creatures and
people dashing on errands,
welcoming them with a singer's
open-mouthed first note from the heart.
I fight for life
for you to speak, for you to step into
the circle

and tell your story.
That is what my open arms
and my laughter convey
when I see you.


I am young, strong, Julia, innocent and loving
beautiful brown eyes and long black hair, with
    caramel skin
my body is scented with sage and cedar
inside my womb butterflies scatter into the day
my eyelids are crow wings
my pulse a cawing at dawn
        the palm-reader's omens
        of things to come—
there will be rich people who do not like me
because my heart is worthier than their gold,
others will scowl in rage that I lie
when I accuse them of injustice,
but the sun and moon as witness
when I see them pale faced, reclined in their
    coffins
on silk pillows, I will kneel and ask the saints
to carry their souls from one to the other worlds
        safely,
        knowing that the only real journey is truth
        how we get from one truth to greater truth.


I am young,
I cuss, I doubt, I am afraid,
because this gentleness I give to you
is a truth I learned from summer seasons being
    alone
and valuing my heart, this compassion I give

to the drunks, the addicts, the street kids
is like the biblical woman who washed Christ's
   feet and dried them with her hair,
so my journey is me
washing my people's feet, being accused by the
   men of whoring,
serving my man, loving fully,
and all the books and magazine articles written
   to empower
to rise and denounce my men,
rebel against their stupidities would only
leave them alone, would only leave them
   stranded
on their journey, and I am journey keeper
   woman,
I help you to understand your way, that you must
   take it,
that you must fearlessly turn the corner
you most want to ignore
to help you face what you will deny,
that is who I am, you Julia, strong Julia,
lovely Julia . . .
whose black hair weighs heavier than gold
on my shoulders . . .
and my man's hand is always in it, turn over the
   gold,
weighing it, offering it to the sun
sniffing like a coyote
      who senses his ancient roots
and becomes certain in his destiny, fortified in
   his fate,
and then moves on in his journey

toward the creator Spirits
    unfolding his life story . . .
I have always known these things—
my true beauty is practicing my people's ways
teaching them the Spirit song
    that will make them strong men, strong
        me . . .


It is on Saturday nights, when the stars are wide
    apart,
        available to all gypsy women
        and I was all of them—
yes, the young one who spent hours putting on
    makeup
who spoke with her brown eyes,
who brashly used her hand to touch
the way a flamenco dancer's hands strike
    lightning
        in every gesture,
I was that girl with eyeliner, lipstick
that would make red roses envy my erotic glance.
    And I taught
    gangsters how to kiss,
    I taught men who usually held
    chrome plated .45s
    in alleys against an enemy's head
    how to hold a child's hand gently.
I was that girl who leaped up in mother's living
    room
watching Zorba the Greek on TV,
    clapped my hands and yanked my father
    from his chair to dance gypsy style,

while my brothers laughed and my mother
disapproved of my flamboyant, shameless
clapping and hollering . . .
you see, I needed to live
I needed to fill the space of my living with me,
  with engagement,
contributing to those stars in the night sky
with my own light—
    I have always been one
    to weep for heroes and heroines,
    I have always loved priestly gangsters,
    those men and women who defy authority,
    who come out of their skins
    haunted by a need to express
    their rebellion
        by gun, by word, by song
        let there by rebellion—
I am Julia, lover of priests and gangsters,
I dance with loneliness this evening, with the
  notes of accordions
fingers smelling of whiskey and woman's vaginal
  juice
punching the white and black keys somewhere
  in Bulgaria,
in some city where children grow to be men at
  five,
and young girls know love at seven,
    in a cabaret in Indonesia where the streets
    smell of recent war, powder and death and
      lawlessness
    and in this environment,
    the voices that sing, the bodies that dance,
    do so because it may be their last and do so

with all their heart, still dreaming of flutes
somewhere among those stars, this Saturday
    night,
when most people are out on dates,
when if you look out your window, see
    them—
a world of people passing in the night,
but so few look to the sky to see the stars
that I see, that you see, that dancers and bar girls
  and poets
see in faraway countries.
    What do the stars say, why do we gaze at
      them?
    Because, when it has come to our lives,
    the tarot cards have lied,
    the diamonds were false,
    the smiles were contrived,
    because in our hearts we smelled horse
      manure
        and loved it more than money,
        because we are the people who ride at
          night
        on stallions with broken legs,
        we are the people who fly at night
        on wings that have been broken,
        we are the people who have escaped our
          captors
        and never reached our homeland.
So I, Julia, dream of love tonight
I, Julia, am the woman who left you with your
  dreams stacked on the table
weeping in your beer, I, Julia,
was once so beautiful that poets who loved me

*235*

grieved for years with memories of hours we
    shared intimately,
        until their love for me interfered with
            all their loves,
        my face appeared before their lovers'
            faces,
        my hands they held as they held their
            lovers' hands,
        my thighs they opened as they opened
            their woman's thighs,
        my tongue they tasted as they sucked
            their woman's mouth,
because I left each of them with a story
of a woman's heart and what she sees gazing at
    the stars,
yes, what she sees gazing at the stars.


I am Julia, woman of many women, trumpet-
    hearted woman
that maddens the bull, el toro, red-caped woman
bloody sword woman, I am Julia who has cut
    each man's heart in half
and squeezed his blood into my palm like an
    orange and drank it,
for days my sweat smelled of man's blood,
        how our love was a furious life and
            death ritual,
        how in gypsy cantinas late at night
        after glasses of corn whiskey
        I lifted my skirt and rubbed my ass
        and danced,
until all the men turned from their tables and
    cried Bravo!

and the young women just into puberty, glanced
  at me
with hunger in their eyes,
        the hunger of starving thieves
        wanting to share a piece of bread
        I, Julia, was the bread,
the bread broken into a thousand pieces to eat
I, Julia, was the priestess singing mournful dirges
  for the dead
I, Julia, was the dove at dawn celebrating a
  child's birth
        I, Julia,
        am woman of many women
am voices harmonizing, am thrashing river
  currents joining,
am the worn guitar lonely fingers have cried
  their passion out on,
am woman giving you myself
    in a hundred different ways
    and in the way tonight I give you myself
    is in these stars, these stars in the sky,
    gaze at them, go to your window and gaze
    step outside and gaze,
    pause and look up,
        and see Julia . . .
        woman of many women
        see Julia . . .

# This Disgusting War!

There's a madness in me this morning—
feels like I have two hands on each side of my
    face,
I'm a young colt for the first time with a saddle
    on my back
and my eyes are maddened with rage and fear
and I'm tossing and yanking my head back
from these two hands
that keep trying to put a bridle on me,
      nor do I want a harness
      around my head!
I want to kick, scream, run and out gallop
the fucking wind.

But the molten lead slowly hardens around my
    bones
and the cry of freedom in me
keeps racing down my arms—*can't get out here,*
the cry hurls itself against my chest—I can't get
    out of my head,
it scurries up my neck—can't get out here,
      and I know what it is
times like these I want to open a bottle of mescal

and pour a nice large drink in the afternoon
    heat
and sit back on a bench somewhere in Arizona
snug my cowboy hat down so the brim shades
    out sunlight
and shoot rattlesnakes all afternoon,
        shoot at cars passing; shoot at hawks and
            eagles and vultures circling above
        shoot at INS prowling the border for
            Mexicans,
spit black tobacco at my boot tips
and shoot the scorpion trying to climb up my
    pants,
then heel crush a tarantula—
        this feeling is the gift the Universe gave me,
        the desperate need to express myself,
the audacity and gall to think I have the right
to call down the Gods and face them, confront
    them, defy their rule,
question why they made this world in the way
    they did,
        not understanding any of it,
the cry in my bones, encased in hardened lead
    so it can't escape,
the cry in my toes that have walked so many
    paths,
the cry in my loins that have fucked so many
    passionate women,
the cry in my mouth that has spoken so many
    prayers,
the cry in my hands that touched so many
    beautiful things,
the cry in my eyes that had seen such violence,

the cry, the Horrifying, All-Engulfing, DARK cry
that cries out to God and Creator and Universe
    why did you take my brother,
        why did you murder my parents
        why did you allow those children in the
            orphanage to be raped,
        why did you allow those innocent men
            in prison to die
        in their spirits,
why
must you Universe crush and smash and destroy
    what is beautiful
give so little understanding—
I defy you, turn my back on you and weep the
    human cry
weep the heart-choking cry, throat-gripping,
    lung-constricting
weep for those you didn't give a damn about!


    If ever God gave me the courage to hold
        court,
        I'd send those Pentagon generals to hell
        stuff a billion dollars up the asses of the
            Defense Department contractors
        and float them off the shores of the Pacific,
because if you don't know how to feel
    compassion
if you've been smugly pampered in your
    moneyed privilege
if you think you're better because of your
    billions and never knew
the fear of not having money to pay for food and
    utility bills,

if your life has been a Tom Cruise/Britney
    Spears carousel ride,
if life never challenged you because mama and
    papa
napkin you every time you spilled milk down
    your chin
if you can lie and cheat and cynically sneer at
    the less fortunate,
        I'd love to shoot you,
        I'd love to cage you up and starve you
        I'd love to bed you down with scorpions
        and corrupt senators for a month,
        not feed you a thing, not hear you cry
            pleading screams,
        dismiss you as a human being,
        tease with electrocution, not enough to kill
            you,
            but keep you shaking and screaming
and I say this,
because you are accountable for countless
    murders and rapes
you have spawned on this land an evil that
    continually seeds new evil
in innocent children, in the streets, in homes, in
    schools,
in fields, in the air, in the heart, in the soul
until even religious leaders and presidents have
    become
evil prophets millions bow down before in
    terror—

I can't
    I can't! I can't!
endure the killing of Palestinians, Iraqis,
  Bosnians, Serbs,
Israelis, Latin Americans, Africans
we are burning Afghani women alive; we are
  assassinating millions
    of innocent people
we are killing millions with each spoonful of
  cereal,
with each spa massage, with each trip to a ski
  resort,
with each Olympic medal we celebrate, with
  each daily paper we read,
    and that's what this cry is in me,
    the one I can't get out,
    the one that haunts me, makes me want to
      lose myself in drugs and alcohol
      because when I walk down the street and see
      no one cares
    that we're murdering millions,
    because when I look from my table and see
      lunch crowds all babbling
about love
and money and spouting happy-blissful new-age
  healing talk,
I want to rise and smoke the motherfuckers,
take them to where their corporate
  consciousness has never taken them,
out of their nice investment portfolios
and comfortable house slippers,
out of their SUVs, out of their lake retreats and
  grad school classrooms

and career moves and Canyon Road Santa Fe
   mansions,
      take them and make them live the life of a
         small starving Mexican girl
one day,
live the life of a woman sold into slavery one day,
live the life of an Afghani woman or Iraqi child,
live the life of someone in jail, in prison, who
   just lost their soul
to men that raped them,
      then let's hear their talk, let's hear their
         jovial laughter come from
those contorted mouths
still agape with horror . . .
      cuz I can't take it anymore,
      just can't
         take this cry in my ears and eyes and mouth
         with the blood of millions of nameless
            victims
all for the pleasure and greed of a few rich
   motherfucking men
gathering in British hotels, Washington
   chambers or Pentagon Think Tanks,
      can't take it . . .
      so I must now play this flute given me by a
         friend now dead,
            I must play this flute, drown out the
               cries of the murdered,
            I must dance my ballet, move so I sweat
               and worm and twist
            and leap and gasp with passionate
               breath,

I must blow this saxophone so hard my
   face reddens
and my cheeks balloon out, eyelids
   tight, blow man blow man!
I must paint in my studio, walk in with
   rage and paint this madness into
love, dance this madness into tears,
   write this poem so I can stop weeping
and start dancing in the community with
   children, women and men,
so I can open with mouth and vociferate my love
   vowels clearly,
so I can use these arms to really bang my hands
   together to applaud
so I can whimsically whirl in a dizzying joy for
   being alive and
against praise the Creator for this life.

# Against Despair

I carry in me a fire,
I dance as flames dance, speak as flames speak
I touch as flame touches, yearn as flame yearns
dream as a flame does,
 and yet,
  you bring water to douse me
  you bring wet wood to warm us
  you wear fire-retardant clothing
  you do not sing the light that flames give
  you moan from the burn
  you do not hum the heat up in your heart
  you let the flame grow gray with morning ice
  the flame cracks from neglect
  like a black butterfly's wing pinned under
   glass.

I rub this heart of mine each morning
I blow on it,
I ask it questions I wrap it in deer hide
I throw dirt over it
I ask it to remember the pain
I tell it to be humble,
I instruct it to be like the mallard ducks
I saw yesterday,

the male one flying north, its female mate
following—
    I told my heart
    learn that lesson well
    go into this day
    smelling of cedar smoke, garden soil, and
      working hands,
    lose your soul in these green sage days
    lose your heart in this Quetzal green day
        on your own unique flight
        to your own primordial map
        tell them who ask
        you are following your joy.


People have accused me of everything,
pile my table with platters of their rage
manipulate words to cheese for laboratory mice
addicted to spiritless pleasures,
leave their complaints at my door
landlord notes for overdue rent,
their disdain disguised in a mask of empathy and
   concern,
remind me of my failures
lavish over my mistakes
excavate the bones of my past—
they will not forget
my thirst for destruction,
daydream to satiate their self-righteousness
cutting off the toes of ballet dancers,
chopping fingers off guitar players,
strangling cellists with cello strings,
they do not seek lover who are free

but those who wear a key around their necks;
       they have the answers;
show them a handsome face and they will kiss it
a muscular body and they will fuck it,
your sadness and they will mock you
your compassion and they will be cynical,
recite a poem and they will try to change it
or shout you down
offer up your heart and they will try to change it
give yourself as you are—they will not accept
    you.


They will tell you that your words are hammers
    pounding them down,
your hopes mere fantasies to enrapture an
    immature heart
that you no longer dream of life as life can offer
    itself
in its splendid magnificence,
but that your needs are selfish
your emotions whimsical, your honesty a well
    camouflaged lie,
and after all of this has been leveled at you,
like myself, countless times,
       I have put on my jacket
strolled to the Rio Grande bosque
seeking counsel from the waters, whispering a
    prayer
for an ancestor appear in the air
beneath my prayer tree (a female cottonwood)
that leans over a green rainbow
under which I stand pray—
I want answers that come from the Creator,

answers to rise from the ground
like Christ on Easter Sunday,
remove the stone from my heart,
        that I might rise from my own death
        to sing my own butterfly metamorphosis
as I change and ascend
winged jewel resting on the twig or leaf a
    moment
        sacrificing myself to the wind and sun
        and by day's end lie dead in dust
        having fulfilled my song.

# ACKNOWLEDGMENTS

I want to thank Jennifer Gates, my agent, what a superb literary eye and sharp mind—thank you so much for believing in my work. Also, my gratitude to Corinna Barsan, what a great delight to work with her, how lucky I am to have such an unrivaled editor. Also to Cindy Bellinger, one of her last acts before dying of cancer was to sit with my Mariposa Letters and excerpt the gems she thought valuable. I consider her sensibility to be in its God-depth of perception for meaning and worth, balanced as it is between this world and the realm beyond. And to Lucia and Esai, my youngest children, and my amazing wife, Stacy, without their support and faith there'd be no book. They believe. Time spent away from them is time spent away from love. To my agent, my editor, and to them I owe this book.

# CREDITS

Grateful acknowledgment is made to the editors and publishers of the following periodicals, chapbooks, and books where poems from this collection first appeared:

*The Dark Horse:* "This Voice Within Me," "Looking"

*Illuminations:* "Excerpt from Letter to Will Inman," "Quetzal Feathers," "Things Unexplained"

*La Roca:* "December Nights"

*Mother Jones:* "Saturday"

*The Sun:* "Silver Water Tower," "With My Massive Soul I Open," "A Handful of Earth, That Is All I Am," "Tapestry of Downtown," "Black Mare," "New Day"

Poems from *Swords of Darkness* originally published by Mango Publishing (1981; Gary Soto, editor).

Poems from *What's Happening* originally published by Curbstone Press (1982).

Poems from *Rockbook 3* originally published by Rock Bottom Books (1978).

Poems from *Set This Book On Fire!* originally published by Cedar Hill Publications (1999; Chris P., editor).

"Smoking Mirrors" originally published in *Que Linda La Brisa* by University of Washington Press (2000).

"Rita Falling from the Sky" was written for *Rita of the Sky*, a documentary by Kathryn Ferguson (2009) and originally published in *Rita and Julia* by San Diego City Works Press (2008).

"Julia," "This Disgusting War!", and "Against Despair" originally published in *Rita and Julia* by San Diego City Works Press (2008).

"Singing at the Gates" originally published in *Descendants*, in collaboration with photographer Norman Mauskopf, by Twin Palms Publishers (2011).